D0218817

Educating the **Gifted** and **Talented**

Resource Issues and Processes for Teachers

Second Edition

**Catherine Clark and
Ralph Callow**

David Fulton Publishers
London

David Fulton Publishers Ltd
The Chiswick Centre, 414 Chiswick High Road, London W4 5TF

www.fultonpublishers.co.uk

First published in Great Britain by David Fulton Publishers in 1998 as *Educating Able Children*

Second edition 2002

The right of Catherine Clark and Ralph Callow to be identifed as the authors of this work has been asserted by them in accordance with the Copyright, Designs and Patents Act 1988.

Copyright © Catherine Clark and Ralph Callow 2002

British Library Cataloguing in Publication Data
A catalogue record for this book is available from the British Library

ISBN 1 85346 873 8

All rights reserved. No part of this publication may be reproduced, stored in a retrieval system or transmitted, in any form, or by any means, electronic, mechanical, photocopying, recording or otherwise, without the prior permission of the publisher.

Typeset by Textype Typesetters, Cambridge
Printed in Great Britain by The Cromwell Press Ltd, Trowbridge, Wiltshire

Contents

Preface

When we were asked to write a second edition of *Educating Able Children: Resource Issues and Processes for Teachers* we both felt that we wanted to emphasise throughout the importance of the idea of 'education'. In *Educating the Gifted and Talented* the issues and processes we describe are therefore contextualised within a framework which sees schools as more than places where the curriculum is delivered and teachers as more than clients who require training in the way that, for instance, some technicians are trained. We have attempted to bring humanistic and holistic approaches back into the education equation as well as democratic first principles for both teachers and their pupils. We think this will encourage the teaching profession to become a learning profession as the Department for Education and Science (DfES) advocates and in doing this the education of gifted and talented pupils will improve.

With this in mind we make comment on the current educational context and initiatives for gifted and talented education which we trust will stimulate discussion and debate. We examine ways of working within the system which encourage flexibility and creativity in both teaching and learning. We also suggest some new ideas for ways forward as well as reworking and, in some cases, restating ideas, techniques and strategies from the first edition which we found it impossible to improve on.

Similarly many of our references were in our last book but are included, alongside new references, because we feel they are still important and useful.

Gifted and talented pupils have never been higher up the education agenda than they are currently. This is potentially an exciting time to be involved in gifted and talented education. We hope this book helps all teachers to make full use of the positive attitude towards celebrating excellence engendered within the educational establishment which has been long awaited. Our aim is to encourage and enable teachers to exploit their own gifts and talents to the full and rise to the challenges involved in educating gifted and talented pupils. By doing so gifted and talented pupils will develop the great potential they all undoubtedly possess.

Catherine Clark
Ralph Callow
March 2002

CHAPTER 1

A critique of the current educational experience of gifted and talented pupils

It must be admitted that the 'cause' of the 'able' or 'gifted' child has never had a great impact on the majority of teachers. Their needs are not so obvious as those, for example, of the slow learner or the disruptive child and, while lacking a great emotional appeal, their case has often been rejected by many by arguments of 'equality' and fairness. 'Why give more to those who are already well endowed?' has been the basis of this attitude. The Third Report of the House of Commons Select Committee on Highly Able Children (1999) addresses this problem, and sets out very clearly that:

> ... they are entitled to have their needs addressed as much as any other child. The commonly held view that they can get by on their own is not borne out by the evidence ... there is ... a significant association between good provision for the most able in the school and for all the children in the school ... many of the strategies which work well for able pupils will also benefit other pupils ... if the school is providing opportunities intended to identify and challenge the highly able, children are more likely to display their latent abilities.

The Report then goes on to specify the main failings of current provision in schools:

1. The needs of children of high ability are not seen as a priority by teachers and schools.
2. Schools do not set high enough levels of expectation of their pupils.
3. The ethos of schools (and more widely society) does not value high academic or intellectual achievement.
4. Teachers are unsure about the most effective ways of recognising high potential or of teaching the most able children.
5. Resources for providing the best education for such children are not available.
(DfES 4 August 2001)

These problems are not new, nor have they been suddenly discovered. Every project concerned with the able child over the last 30 years, whether national or local, has tried to address some or all of them.

In spite of the repeated claims that standards in education are rising, it is hard to believe that the present prospects for the able child, or indeed any other child, are particularly bright; and that the true 'failings' cannot be adequately addressed in the near future, whatever new elements are bolted on to the present school system.

The teachers

In the last year 26,000 trained teachers left the profession. Of the newly qualified teachers, 60% left within the first three years of teaching. There is strong anecdotal evidence to suggest that if the retirement regulation had not been made much stricter many of their older colleagues would have left as well. Certainly many head teachers and senior members of staff will readily admit they are 'serving their time' until the earliest moment when they can retire without losing their rights to a pension. The loss of newly qualified teachers means that, in cash terms, £100 million of tax-payers' money is spent each year on training for people who take the first opportunity to leave a profession which they find unrewarding, not only in monetary terms but in job satisfaction and fulfilment (*Times Educational Supplement* 2 November 2001).

In addition, many potentially good teachers are not coming forward. The ability of men entering the teaching profession is, on average, significantly lower than it was in the 1970s (*TES* 19 October 2001). Many good candidates of both sexes are excluded by the deeply flawed and ludicrous skill tests in numeracy, literacy and information and communication technology (ICT) (*TES* 2 November 2001). There is also evidence that older teachers are actively discouraging their children from entering the profession (*TES* 19 October 2001).

The facts are that many are leaving before they have acquired much classroom experience and many, who would in the past have been highly effective teachers, are simply not being recruited.

There are a number of reasons for this quite dramatic haemorrhage of staff: 'It looks as if many have got ground down by the changes in the profession' (according to Professor Smithers who carried out the research); they had 'gone into teaching as a vocation and it has become a more individual process, where they were judged by output' (*TES* 2 November 2001).

This shortage of staff can only place extra burdens on senior teachers, already struggling with mountains of administrative documents. It is, therefore, becoming increasingly unlikely that any group of children with special needs will profit from a situation where a large proportion of the teachers is inexperienced, or of a lower intellectual capacity. The Head of Ofsted (Office for Standards in Education) 'expects to see a growing mismatch – the number of teachers (in secondary schools) teaching subjects for which they are not qualified', so a lack of subject-specific expertise could be added to lack of experience.

The curriculum

The National Curriculum was '. . . a deliberate attempt [by the Tories] to put teachers in their place'.

> . . . Any doubts I had that the main players in the education game had the remotest interest in children, classrooms and teachers were dispelled.
> (Duncan Graham, 1981–91 Chairman and Chief Executive of the National Curriculum Council, in the *Guardian* 22 October 2001)

The National Curriculum, with its highly specific programmes of learning, detailed targets and vast size and detail, is a prescription for educational disaster; a stultifying exercise in futility which limits the intellectual horizons of teacher and child, generates immense amounts of paper records and frustrates the enthusiasm and spirit of the teacher.

> Teaching as a profession should be for people with imagination. The ability to invent and create is precious: the badge of the true professional. It must be protected like the Crown Jewels. Take away imagination and we have teacher-as-machine, programmed androids, not humans with a heart beat. (*TES* 13 July 2001)

Did the people who introduced the system fear the effect of unrestricted learning on the masses; that it would make them 'too clever by half – clever enough to see through their political masters?

Certainly this system – which in its earlier manifestation, the Revised Code of 1862, proved barely adequate for the nineteenth century – is woefully inadequate for the twenty-first century. In the last analysis it is a vast and expensive exercise in political and bureaucratic paranoia – which clearly demonstrates that the professionals are not to be trusted to do the job they were so carefully trained for. The sad fact is that for many children and teachers it is too late:

> We can't undo the damage that we have done in the last decade or two . . .
> (*Guardian* 30 October 2001)

In the past many young minds found intellectual nourishment in the public libraries, and knowledge and stimulation for the imagination in radio and television programmes. This is still the case but how many children are frustrated by the mindless drivel which is pumped out in sound and vision by a 'dumbed down' television service and the empty shelves in public libraries due to financial cut-back? Even in the local bookshops you will find dull ranks of crammers, home coaching books for the national tests edging out the copies of *Harry Potter* and *The Hobbit*.

Assessment

> Education. SAT: . . . the acronym for the tests that were now given every school child in the country . . . the ultimate analysis of a test . . . that had been devised by the mediocre to advance the mediocre through a common educational system . . . (Vidal 2000: 440)

We are constantly being told that school standards are rising. This statement is based largely on children's scores in the school attainment tests. The figures always sound very impressive but what is the validity of the tests, and at what cost were the results achieved?

The sad truth, borne out by empirical and anecdotal evidence, is that teachers are forced by pressures inside and outside their schools to spend inappropriate amounts of time in coaching for the school tests (*TES* 2 November 2001). Poetry, drama and art are set aside so that lessons can be devoted to learning 'to regurgitate phrases to improve writing scores' or memorising facts in science. Whether the children actually learn anything of value during this process is debatable; what is, however, quite clear is that there is a very noticeable drop in enthusiasm for those subjects that are crammed (*TES* 19 August 2001).

The frightful shambles which was caused by the introduction of the AS levels in secondary schools reveal just how test-mad the system has become. The voluntary associations help teacher and parent where they can and there are still devoted teachers who are, in spite of all the problems, struggling to 'educate' their pupils. There will, thank heavens, always be teachers of their calibre; but their task is getting no easier.

Conclusion

If our schools are to become places where all our children can be happy, safe, inspired and become wise, the system must change. There must be a fundamental overhaul of the curriculum and examinations for all pupils. Testing must be reduced and altered in its form and methodology, and government must learn to trust its teachers.

Reform would be a highly complex and delicate operation demanding adequate resources and time to accomplish it – will any government have the courage to attempt it, or will they continue to parrot the comforting mantra of 'rising standards' and simply bolt on the gifted and talented programme as another 'initiative'?

> The pernicious transformation of education into a consumer commodity and of schools and universities into secular temples of commercial values – modularisation and the mechanical assessment it demands – is no accident. That transformation – instigated by a Tory party fearful of 'the great unwashed' and furthered beyond its wildest dreams by the Neo-liberal determination of New

Labour fundamentalists to produce a docile workforce and not an increasingly critical electorate – has been quite deliberate. (*Times Higher Educational Supplement* 1 February 2002).

Far from draining the swamp, all they will do is throw in more alligators!

References

House of Commons Education and Employment Committee (1999) Third Report, 'Highly Able Children'. London: HMSO.

Vidal, G. (2000) *The Golden Age*. London: Little, Brown & Co.

CHAPTER 2

How to make best use of the current initiatives for gifted and talented pupils

The challenge for teachers of gifted and talented pupils remains, as always, how to do their best for these pupils in spite of political change and fundamental problems and difficulties within the education system.

The following anecdote provides a dramatic illustration of what some teachers were up against just 15 years ago:

> I ran a course entitled 'Working with Able Children in the Primary Classroom' in 1987. There were 25 places available but we had to squeeze in five extra people because there was so much interest. Having introduced myself, I did what I usually did and went around the group asking everyone to say, briefly, who they were, where they taught and why they had come on the course. After about ten people had introduced themselves, the next teacher hesitated before speaking. I thought she was taking time to clear her throat but she wasn't. When she spoke she said her name and why she had come along but she also said 'I'm sorry I'm a bit wary of saying which school I work at because officially my LEA does not recognise the term "able child" and they have not supported me on this course. My Head agreed that I could come if I paid for myself which is what I have done. But officially I should not be attending this course.' There was a surprised reaction in the room. Then it emerged that several teachers from other LEAs were in the same position.

Hopefully no teacher would find themselves in that position today. Times have undoubtedly changed but the question is whether they have changed for the better.

Some would argue the future for clever pupils has never looked brighter than it does at the moment. To start with there is a new official term to describe them – 'gifted and talented'. It is perhaps indicative of the confused thinking in this country about the education of gifted and talented pupils that several different descriptions were used in reports in the 1980s and 1990s including 'able', 'more able' and 'high achievers'. Each provoked intense debate because they impacted on the beliefs, values and assumptions of educationalists about this emotive issue with its elitist connotation. Freeman (1998) comments that worldwide there must be about one hundred different descriptions and definitions, each of which have their own nuances and ambiguities which potentially can create problems. For instance, she comments that 'gifted and talented' carries with it a connotation of gifts being dispensed from on high. Nevertheless two years ago the DfES decided on the term 'gifted and talented' and from January 2000 it has been used in the Ofsted Framework for the Inspection of Schools.

In government documentation, therefore, 'gifted' refers to pupils with high ability or potential in academic subjects and 'talented' refers to those with high ability or potential in the expressive or creative arts or sports.

In the Excellence in Cities Initiative (EiC) it is expected that all schools will list at a ratio of 2:1 gifted to talented pupils.

The change in attitude of the educational establishment towards these pupils has gone a lot further than a name change. Following the publication of the Third Report of the Education and Employment Committee in 1999 on Highly Able Children, the Government, as part of the Excellence in Cities Initiative which aims to raise performances in schools, included a strand for gifted and talented pupils. To date, February 2002, EiC covers one third of all schools. It is estimated that £300 million pounds will be spent between 2003 and 2004 on the EiC Initiative as a whole. The Government clearly means business and for the first time, gifted and talented pupils are an integral part of that whole.

As Deborah Eyre, Chief Training Provider at Westminster College, says:

> It is wonderful that we have a major initiative which is looking systematically at the education of the gifted and talented. (*EiC Newsletter* 10 October 2001)

Stephen Timms, Schools Standards Minister at the DfES, said:

> It is a mistake to assume that gifted and talented children can develop themselves. Many are achieving against the odds and there are many more who are not yet identified. We owe them the right mix of challenge and support. (*The Times* 14 October 2001)

What is being done for gifted and talented pupils?

1. Reformation of the examination system

Part of this 'right mix' is the decision by the Secretary of State for Education, Estelle Morris, to reform the examination system in order, as she said, to:

> set high achievers free from the rigid structures that have held them back in the past. (*The Times* 12 February 2002)

To be introduced after consultation in 2004, the aim is to encourage the brightest pupils to take GCSEs early and skip this examination altogether in their strongest subjects going straight on to AS levels.

The plan is that this will leave these students more time

- to pursue other interests in the sixth form; or
- study new subjects such as Psychology or Archaeology; or
- take a gap year.

First responses from head teachers have indicated they would need reassurance that the universities would be prepared to use the AS framework for university entrance requirements. John Dunford, of the Secondary Heads Association, has commented that he does not expect that this will result in large numbers of pupils taking GCSEs early; people will opt for safety (*The Times* 12 February 2002).

The DfES has also suggested further reforms in the examination system at A level. For those who obtain two A levels and an AS level, an *Advanced Award* should be given while those who obtain three A levels at ABB plus an AS level should be given a *Higher Award*.

There is also a possibility that at A grade at Advanced level the difference between an A and an A* would be based on the candidate answering extra questions.

First responses to this proposal, particularly the A/A* distinction, have been sceptical saying that it is both impractical and confusing. The Government hope that it would go some way to bolster up the A level as the gold standard qualification. The question is would it help gifted and talented students?

COMMENT

We feel that it needs to be said that Estelle Morris's quotation about rigid structures holding gifted and talented pupils back applies mostly to state schools. Independent schools have for many years encouraged their best pupils to take public examinations early. It is surely an indictment of the way that the comprehensive school movement in general developed during the 1970s and 1980s that this was allowed to happen. It was not necessary. The system was, in theory, always flexible enough to allow students to take subjects early. In many cases it was the teachers and head teachers, afraid to lay themselves open to the criticism of elitism, who prevented this from happening.

Indeed in the 1960s I taught in some schools where academic attainment was exclusively downplayed and only prowess in sport, drama or music was applauded: this in the mistaken belief by staff that they were levelling the playing field to remove any advantage that pupils with academic ability might have had. These half-understood concepts, wrongly believed to underpin comprehensive education, resulted in the kind of crude response which particularly ill-served gifted pupils. But to what extent – in an environment where everybody was to be the same as everyone else and nobody was to stand out from anyone else – did this affect those with great talent also?

How far have schools come since the 1970s and 1980s?

To what extent have they accepted the challenge of valuing and educating gifted and talented pupils appropriately?

How much flexibility have schools built into the system for gifted and talented pupils?

What is their attitude towards gifted and talented pupils?

Within the last three years there has been a sea change in official thinking. This Government now positively encourages schools to put in place identification procedures to ascertain who has ability or potential ability. It is seen as essential to provide appropriate support for these pupils. The clear message is that the Government believes this country will not prosper unless the potential of our most able pupils is cultivated.

2. *The Academy for Gifted and Talented Youth*

Warwick University, together with Oxford Brookes University partnered by Johns Hopkins University in the USA, has been awarded a contract to run a summer academy for our brightest teenagers aged 11–16. The residential courses lasting for up to three weeks will cater for the top 5–10% of the school population. The first will take place in 2002. Initially there will be 600 places rising to 900 by 2003 by which time the age range may have been extended to 19 years of age. Additional support is to be given to parents and teachers and there will be online provision for the students themselves.

There is a suggestion that the top 1 per cent might have separate provision from the rest of the students in the form of a postgraduate tutor. During the pilot summer school in July 2002 a choice of three subjects will be on offer: there will be an accelerated maths course and courses in arts and the humanities. Although poor parents will not be expected to pay fees, better off parents will be expected to do so. It is predicted that the cost will be several hundred pounds.

The intention is to condense a year's worth of high school study into three weeks but Warwick University insists that there will be no 'hothousing or fast tracking'. The students' well-being in all ways will come first.

This project is intended by Government to counteract to some extent poor parenting and poor teaching. They are encouraging students from the worst schools to attend.

The Academy was described by Stephen Timms, the Schools Minister, as:

> the centrepiece of our national strategy to support and improve gifted and talented education. We ignore the needs of our most able young people at our peril. (*The Times* 24 February 2002)

COMMENT

While the Academy may well succeed in its aims, underlying problems within the education system also need to be tackled systematically so that the benefits for students attending the Academy are not lost. The real success of the Academy will depend upon whether the education system as a whole, through EiC or other initiatives, is able to make the necessary changes so that the gap between what is experienced at the Academy and in school is lessened.

It may well be unrealistic to expect schools to provide the level of expertise which presumably will be available at the Academy but schools *can* manage and organise learning experiences for gifted and talented pupils to allow them to forge ahead at their own pace.

They can work on teacher-pupil relationships in a new way so that both see each other as a resource, working in partnership in the learning process.

They can make sure that gifted and talented pupils have longer spells of time to spend on topics so that they can widen and deepen the learning experience.

They can give these pupils a chance to work in a more sustained way over time.

All of these things, and there are many other examples, are within the realms of possibility for any school if there is the willingness to consider gifted and talented pupils as a priority.

The second issue regarding the Academy which requires comment concerns the way in which students are to be identified as being in the top 1%, 5% or 10% and thus chosen for the Academy.

Parents, children and schools are being asked to nominate potential students for the pilot scheme. David VandeLinde, the Vice Chancellor of Warwick University, says that there will also be 'some sort of specially devised entrance exam'. However, it is well known that the whole issue of testing for ability and particularly potential ability is problematic.

The world-class test launch in 2001 to identify the top 10% of the ability range in maths and problem solving is only at the earliest stage. The hope is to attain international benchmarks and therefore agreement about identification in the USA, New Zealand, Australia, Hong Kong and Britain.

This cause for concern is not a reason for not running the Academy but it raises an issue which urgently requires further consideration. We need to ensure that the best possible techniques are in place to identify gifted and talented pupils in schools as well as for the Academy.

3. *Subsidising places at independent schools*

The philanthropist Peter Lampl has had a long-standing interest in supporting gifted and talented pupils. His most recent venture has been to subsidise places at a well-known and highly respected independent school, Belvedere, for girls from families where parents or guardians are unemployed or not well off. In this scheme the intake has to comprise 20% of girls whose parents are unemployed and 30% blue and white collar workers who could not otherwise afford the school fees.

The head teacher maintains that it would be hard for anyone to pick these girls out from any others in their year group. It will, however, be interesting to see how the cohort performs when they come to take public examinations. It is also worth noting that some full fee-paying parents have removed their daughters from the school since this scheme began.

COMMENT

The Lampl scheme is, of course, the assisted places scheme under a different name. The assisted places scheme was discontinued for financial as well as political reasons by this

Government about five years ago. It is ironic, therefore, that just a few years later a number of schemes similar to the Lampl scheme have been allowed to take root. Certainly there are no financial implications for the Government with such schemes. Is finance, therefore, the principle which demands first consideration by the Government when making decisions about education? In terms of first political principles, should there not be a problem for the Government with this scheme which promotes independent schools?

The Lampl scheme at Belvedere School raises a number of other issues for us. For instance, at what point is the balance within a school system disturbed to the extent that it no longer works well and indeed cannot work well? When does it become impossible for the management, organisation and teaching systems to function effectively and efficiently? At Belvedere 50% of the intake are to be subsidised and 50% full fee paying. Is this the right balance? On what are these percentages based? Common sense? Are they right?

We know of a secondary school in the North East of England with a mixed catchment which established itself as a high achieving school. It also had an excellent reputation for caring for pupils. As a result, parents without the catchment area started to send their children to this school. Because of its reputation it attracted a high proportion of children with a wide range of special educational needs.

After a few years the school could not cope with the intake in the way that it had done previously; it was overwhelmed by the influx of pupils with educational and social problems and did not have the resources to cope because the children with special needs came with the minimum of support from the LEAs.

Five years later this school, where much that was described as good practice had been observed, and where innovative approaches to education such as Thinking Skills had successfully been introduced across the school, failed its Ofsted inspection.

The key issue is: What is the right balance in a school population in terms of ability, sex, race, culture, creed or class to ensure that pupils are educated appropriately?

This leads us on to consider the broader related issue of how to provide a suitable education for gifted and talented pupils. What is the right balance for them?

What kinds of environments encourage these pupils to flourish? We need to look again at what the environments might comprise. It may be necessary to take some hard decisions about ways forward. We have to focus on questions such as:

- Can it always be helpful for gifted and talented pupils to be in a minority, sometimes a tiny minority?
- Can it be expected that all schools will be able to meet the needs of gifted and talented pupils?
- Should there be more special schools especially for gifted children?
- Are subsidised places in independent schools a way forward?

These are all contentious issues which bring up questions about inclusion which have beset special needs education over many years. There are no easy answers but this does not mean that they ought not to be discussed especially at a time when schools are operating in an increasingly litigious climate. For example, there has been a case recently in which an independent school was taken to court by a student who did not get the predicted A grade at A level (*The Sunday Times* 7 October 2001). Hopefully this is not the main reason why schools would want to improve their record regarding gifted and talented pupils but it is one facet of the culture of accountability in which we live and of which we would be prudent to take heed.

4. Different approaches to teacher development

The latest official thinking about development opportunities for teachers of gifted and talented pupils is that there ought to be a wider range of development opportunities on offer.

One suggestion is that teachers should be given bursaries, for example to explore work-based learning with time for collaboration, sharing and reflection. Other ideas include:

- teachers being given sabbaticals;
- teachers from beacon schools, specialist schools and specialist advanced skills teachers having time to share thinking and experiences with teachers in ordinary schools;
- peer networks, clusters working together;
- professional working teams in which teachers work together over a period of time on issues that interest them.

Some teachers have received bursaries for best practice research scholarships to investigate topics such as how gifted and talented students perform in mixed-ability groups. Teacher exchanges between, for instance, ordinary school and beacon school for either short visits, demonstration lessons or longer visits have been suggested.

International exchanges and study visits are also included in the range of possibilities, as are virtual teacher centres in which ICT is the main focus of contact. The latter are in the early stage of development.

Professional development through partnerships between EiC schools and independent schools is also recommended; possible models include:

- residential projects
- working with undergraduates and gifted and talented pupils
- involvement in Education Action Zones
- workshops
- Masterclasses
- mentoring partnerships
- staffing partnerships
- homework clubs.

The DfES is keen to hear the views of teachers about these options. Obviously no one way forward will suit all but at least with variety comes choice and this has to be a welcome change in professional development where usually there has been little or none for teachers. It is very important that more teachers are able to educate gifted and talented pupils to a high standard.

Monitoring done thus far on the gifted and talented strand of EiC has indicated, in some ways not surprisingly, that the essential ingredients for educating gifted and talented pupils successfully are:

- enthusiasm and committed coordination at all levels – school, cluster and partnership
- an ability for lead coordinators to influence the school, for which they need:
  - time to do the job
  - to be able to access key people within the school
  - support from senior management.

COMMENT

Many of these examples require teachers to collaborate, share and reflect together. What strikes us is the lack of comment on a difficulty which will most likely result from such activities: that is the dilemma of sharing in the highly competitive world in which we live.

However desirable in theory it may be to be altruistic and care for others, in reality will this happen? For instance, how will teachers who teach in a school that is highly successful with gifted and talented pupils feel about cooperating with teachers from a school that is not?

Surely it is only natural that teachers will want to protect the status and standing of their own school for league table purposes if not for any other. Yet they are being asked to share their expertise within the cluster or partnership which may adversely affect that school's ability to attract gifted and talented pupils. They may even be expected to work over a substantial period of time with colleagues who have very little idea of how to work with gifted and talented students. Where does altruism stop? What is in it for those teachers and schools that appear to be giving more than they are receiving?

Such issues, understandably in our view, will be floating around either on the surface or under the surface in cluster groups. They may not be insurmountable but they need to be explored so that all involved feel that as well as giving they are getting something out of the sharing.

Does this parallel the dilemma of gifted children in mixed-ability groups? Do they too give more than they get? Yes, it is nice for them to feel that they belong to a group, most probably they will have a lot to offer to the group and it will be socially less stressful than when working as an individual. Often gifted pupils stick out like a sore thumb because they work longer and harder and they give erudite and thought-provoking answers. The sense of being one of the crowd and reaching out to others is usually pleasant as well as socially desirable, maybe even preferable to some. But what are gifted pupils getting academically from mixed-ability settings and groups? Might mixed-ability settings not lead to a feeling of academic frustration for gifted pupils?

The questions that need to be asked are:

- For what percentage of time should gifted and talented pupils be expected to learn through group work, especially mixed-ability group work?

- Do all pupils, not only gifted pupils, know, with some degree of precision, what it is that they are aiming to achieve, particularly when learning through group work?

Another major issue in the area of professional development which is not discussed at all in the DfES information about professional development is the importance of relationships. No matter what type of development work is done, if the relationships do not feel right, whether it be between specialist teacher and ordinary teacher, gifted and talented coordinator and subject teacher, or lead coordinator and head teacher, then the experience is bound to be affected and usually not for the better.

The necessity in our view to consider very carefully the practical implications of working together before embarking on projects cannot be overstated. This involves:

- having a clear understanding of the role each person is to play and how they might play it
- learning processes
- how as individuals we learn best.

Successful professional development is more than a unique blend of the theoretical and the practical. It is also about the emotions, beliefs, aspirations and experiences of those involved. If the models of professional development currently being considered do not take this into account then they are likely to be less successful than they might be.

Teachers are people first and professionals second.

5. Excellence in Cities: the gifted and talented strand and other grant-funded programmes: ways forward based on the Ofsted Report 2001

The grant-funded programmes, including the gifted and talented strand in EiC, indicate how seriously this Government, following the report of the Select Committee in 1999, is taking the education of gifted and talented pupils. Undoubtedly this is a major step change in government policy. Government is literally beginning to put money and resources into the system in order to make things happen.

Ofsted reported on the early stages of EiC in late 2001. The main conclusions were that:

1. There has overall been an increase in the amount and quality of additional activities, often out of school hours, for gifted and talented pupils.
2. There has been little significant change in the organisation or teaching of mainstream classes.
3. At this point it is too early to see sustained impact on attainment in tests and examinations.
4. There is a need for training to be available to all teachers particularly with regard to subject-specific work.
5. There are some difficulties in identifying pupils for extra activities.

COMMENT

The report mentions that the monitoring of the benefits of additional programmes was rarely evident and that there was little evidence of sustained impact of the additional activities. In other words these activities were very much bolt-on, stand-alone experiences and insufficient effort appears to have been made to link them with ongoing mainstream school activities either through the use of transferable skills or the knowledge base.

This is a worrying phenomenon in our view because it indicates that the teachers involved have not thought through sufficiently what they were doing and why they were doing it, otherwise they would have been aware of the need for continuity and progression from the extra, additional or special activities back into ordinary school life. Was this because they were working under pressure to get the initiatives up and running?

The ultimate aim of any initiative must surely be to transform what goes on in ordinary school life, what happens day by day in classrooms. As all EiC schools are expected to identify between 5% and 10% of their pupils as gifted and talented, no school can say it has no gifted and talented pupils. So all of the schools have an interest in finding a way forward which utilises every available resource to the maximum. What this means is that the focus cannot solely be on extra activities for gifted and talented pupils but needs to be equally on what happens to them during regular lessons.

The report lists the following features of effective practice in identifying high ability:

- articulation and discussion within the school of the characteristics of high ability and potential in subject contexts, including indicators of interest and high level skills in approaches to learning;
- systematic assembly and scrutiny of the available information on performance and potential, including information from screening tests and observation of pupils at work;
- special attention to groups likely to be under-represented in lists based on current attainment because of lack of opportunity or for other reasons;
- clear presentation to pupils and parents of the purpose of identification and the opportunities that are available as a result;
- the involvement of parents and pupils in identifying strengths and interest in activities at school and elsewhere.

We offer more ideas about identification techniques in Chapter 7.

The report also emphasises the importance of teacher assessment as the main component in identifying talented pupils. It is worth noting that the best forms of assessment were done by teachers observing and reflecting on the learning they observed. In Chapter 5 we discuss in more depth ways of observing pupils and analysing the data collected.

The report provides the following useful example of an approach to assessment where astute observation by teachers came up with the following characteristics of pupils who were talented in music:

- They are more attentive than others when music is played, ask questions and want to discuss their own musical experiences.

- They sing tunefully and with enthusiasm, repeating extracts of songs sung with them, and enjoy sharing and revisiting of the experience.
- They are fascinated by the sounds of musical instruments, focus intently when they see and hear them live, volunteer when offered the opportunity to play a musical instrument and are confident to display their skills to the rest of the class.
- They enjoy the composing activity and like to lead the group, looking around the rest of the group and acknowledging when musical entries are made.

Masterclasses

Three types of Masterclass were identified:

- those that offered accelerated study of a subject
- those that sought to develop generic skills
- those that concentrated on broadening understanding.

Often there was an overlap between the three types.

The most effective approach to identifying those who should participate was through testing and the subjective findings of teachers. With reference to ICT the inspectors commented that the pupils could have got much more from the project but because of staff inexperience they did not.

The best Masterclasses were successful in catering for the pupils' gifts and talents but there was little evidence of continuity and progression.

Good lessons were seen, characterised by clear frameworks, high expectations, shared discussion and scope being given for the pupils to develop ideas. But few of the Masterclasses constituted true Masterclasses.

COMMENT

It has to be a matter of concern that some teachers, despite the fact that they had been freed from the constraints of whole-class teaching, were unable to provide a stimulating and challenging learning environment.

It is also worrying that the teachers were not able to teach true Masterclasses. Was this because they did not have the expertise to challenge these high-fliers or was it that they did not know how to use this expertise in that particular situation?

Equally it is worrying that there was little evidence of continuity and progression. Why not? Since the introduction of the National Curriculum no learning programme has been considered to be satisfactory unless both of these aspects have been planned in.

And why in some Masterclasses did pupils finish tasks early and have time on their hands?

Summer schools

Pupils were chosen from Years 6–9 through cognitive ability tests, National Curriculum test results at Key Stage 2 and teacher assessment. Pupils enjoyed themselves at summer schools. They had a positive impact on self-esteem and motivation. However, the long-term benefits were uncertain.

Teaching was generally of a good quality; it generated excitement among the pupils combined with the opportunity to explore new ideas, develop new techniques and acquire knowledge. Pupils commented that teachers at summer school were not like teachers, maybe because many of them were not school teachers. Some of the best teaching on the summer schools was not from school teachers but college lecturers, LEA Advisory Teachers and other experts.

COMMENT

Again these comments ring alarm bells. What are the implications for teachers and schools?

Do teachers know their subject(s) well enough to challenge gifted and talented pupils?

Can teachers join up the experiences of in-school learning with out-of-school learning such that continuity and progression are evident? This is important if in the long term these experiences are going to make a difference to levels of achievement.

What was it about the summer school environment that made the teachers, according to the pupils, behave differently? Did this mean that the pupils learnt more or enjoyed learning more? Are there implications for teachers in school?

In Chapter 5 we discuss the characteristics of successful teachers of the gifted, the styles of teaching that appeal to them and the learning environments in which gifted pupils appear to do well.

Independent/maintained school partnerships

Pupils were nominated and identified by the schools with the focus on groups rather than individuals. The pupils were chosen because they were in a particular year group or set which was studying a specific subject. The emphasis was on deepening or broadening the subject. Thus schools were able to develop their normal curriculum provision and access facilities not otherwise available to them.

Teaching seen was generally very good. There was usually a sense of shared excitement and expectation, variety of pace and activities, and clear objectives. Pupils were overwhelmingly enthusiastic in the independent/maintained school partnerships. It is interesting to note that although the funding for the project has ended, in some cases, the schools have decided to continue to work together.

This programme avoided some of the pitfalls of the Masterclasses and summer schools because it focused on the normal curriculum and looked at ways of extending and enriching that experience. It did not therefore have problems resulting from the bolt-on effect.

COMMENT

No reference is made to the teachers in the independent/maintained school partnerships not having experience to cope with the subject matter. Neither is there any reference to teachers who were not school teachers being involved. Clearly in these partnerships the school teachers themselves were up to the challenge. The interesting question is why?

This model should be looked at more closely because it is the only model in which the gifted and talented pupils were reported as 'overwhelmingly enthusiastic'.

The report provides two tables of particular use, the first about features of effective teaching which were present in the most successful initiatives:

Table 2.1 Findings of the 2001 Ofsted Report

Features of effective teaching
a high degree of subject knowledge
understanding of how to plan class work and homework to increase the pace, breadth or depth of the coverage of the subject
the capacity to envisage and organise unusual projects and approaches which catch pupils' attention and make them want to explore the topic
the use of tasks which help pupils to develop perseverance and independence in learning through their own research and investigation, while ensuring that they have the necessary skills and knowledge to tackle the work effectively on their own
the use of demanding resources which help pupils engage with difficult or complex ideas
the use of ICT to extend and enhance pupils' work and the opportunity to present the outcomes to others
the ability to deploy high-level teaching skills in defining expectations, creating positive classroom climate for enquiry, asking probing questions, managing time and resources, and assessing progress through the lesson
the confidence to try out new ideas, to take risks and to be prepared to respond to leads which look most likely to develop higher levels of thinking by pupils

Among the issues that the report states require attention by the schools in the initiatives are the following:

- improving methods of identification
- engaging parents and pupils
- developing subject-specific approaches
- giving earlier attention to the skills of independent learning
- making the most of additional provision
- recognising the implications for staffing
- improving monitoring
- most importantly, establishing a secure base for improving mainstream school practice.

The second table offers helpful ideas on the effective management of gifted and talented pupils in schools. Among other things it stresses the importance of five conditions (see Table 2.2).

Table 2.2 Conditions for effective pupil management

having a coordinator with a well-defined role
leadership from heads of department on identification, schemes of work and special programmes
a willingness to consider other kinds of organisation for teaching groups
the effective monitoring of individuals and groups
the development of links with other schools to develop good practice

COMMENT

The issues addressed in this report are by no means new; many of them have been raised in the field of gifted and talented education previously and most have been discussed in relation to special needs education over a number of years. The really big question is why so many of the same points are raised with alarming regularity and why they have not been adequately dealt with. Is it merely a question of finance, resource and training or is there more to it than that?

In relation to this report, some of the questions which have occurred to us that may cast light on this all-encompassing question include the following:

- Why in the EiC had schools made little progress in refining monitoring systems to take specific account of work with gifted and talented pupils?
- Why was it that EiC schools found it hard to shape the initiative into whole-school action?
- Why in EiC schools is differentiation underdeveloped?
- Why are teachers generally uncertain about what it is they should be doing with gifted and talented pupils?

Frank discussion about such issues would surely make overt what is covert and in doing so enable schools to make the best use of current initiatives. Such discussion should be part of the professional development process which is the key to unlocking so many of the doors to problems highlighted in this chapter and the reason why it is such a major focus in our book.

References

Freeman, J. (1998) *Educating the Very Able: Current International Research*. London: HMSO.

House of Commons Education and Employment Committee (1999) Third Report, 'Highly Able Children'. London: HMSO.

Office for Standards in Education (Ofsted) (2001) *Providing for Gifted and Talented Pupils: An Evaluation of Excellence in Cities and Other Grant-funded Programmes*. London: The Stationery Office.

CHAPTER 3

A response to the current context based on an integrated model of professional development

The educational context post-1990 with reference to gifted and talented education

Concern about gifted underachievers surfaced again as it has done periodically during the previous three decades when Her Majesty's Inspectorate (HMI) (1992) found that gifted pupils from poor backgrounds were being underserved in mainstream schools. But this was not the whole story.

☛ In the early 1990s the vast majority of gifted pupils in state schools, whatever their home circumstances, were being insufficiently challenged. In 1994 HMI suggested that schools that adequately catered for their gifted pupils generally did better with all pupils.

This assertion raised the profile of gifted education nationally and was one reason why schools took advantage of the National Association for Able Children in Education (NACE)/Department for Education and Employment (DfEE) (1993–6) inservice programme.

Other changes occurred around this time which made schools pay greater attention to the education of their gifted pupils. When schools were inspected the policy, planning and provision made for more able pupils was, in many cases, included under the umbrella of Equal Opportunities. There were insufficient Inspectors with expertise in gifted and talented education which was problematic but nevertheless this was a signal by Government that:

☛ by the mid-1990s it was expected, and therefore it was politically correct, and no longer considered elitist, for schools to identify and provide for more able pupils.

Even ten years previously this had not been the case.

Gifted pupils were given further consideration in *Excellence in Schools* (DfEE 1997) where concern was expressed that many gifted and talented pupils were, despite these additional efforts, still underachieving.

Schools were challenged to think seriously about what they offered these pupils. Ofsted even questioned whether schools that were doing well were, in fact, 'coasting', that is doing well but not well enough by their gifted pupils (Hackett 1998). They challenged these schools to improve outcomes and 'light touch' inspections were undertaken to ensure that they did so. Other initiatives focused on encouraging primary schools to set children so that bright children got the chance to work together.

One of the underlying issues which was raised in this attempt to drive up standards was the *quality* of the education of gifted pupils in ordinary schools. The Department for Education and Employment's Select Committee concluded that these pupils were entitled to have their needs met as much as any other child. It was recommended that each school should identify and challenge their most able pupils. Schools were given guidelines about what to do but had they the wherewithal to do it? For instance, did they have staff who were sufficiently motivated and skilled to do the job?

Mention was made in the guidelines of the importance of making special provision for more able pupils through:

- acceleration
- flexible groupings
- accelerated learning
- thinking skills.

But all of these ways forward made yet further demands on teachers who were already reeling with the many changes in the education system which had occurred over two decades.

Some schools responded well to these suggestions, others did not. However, the buck stopped with the teachers. It was their job to ensure that an appropriate education was offered to all pupils in their care including those with gifts and talents.

The big question was how could teachers be best prepared for the task in hand? This is still being debated today. It is important to find out the best ways of supporting teachers as they seek to provide an appropriate education for gifted and talented pupils.

Taking another look at teacher professional development

In the light of the growing pressure from Government to ensure that gifted and talented pupils in ordinary classrooms are well taught, it is necessary to reconsider the ways in which teachers are prepared to teach. There is general agreement that at present there are insufficient teachers who regard themselves as confident and competent to teach gifted and talented pupils. It is therefore timely with recent government initiatives to look again at what is on offer to teachers who wish to develop such expertise.

As a result of the Excellence in Cities Initiative (EiC) started in 2000 the situation is improving, but there are still few courses specifically focused on gifted and talented pupils, either in initial teacher education or continuing professional development. It is clearly essential for this and other reasons, not least the pressure on teacher time, that any courses on offer are taught effectively and considered to be meaningful and purposive by teachers.

The current drive by Government to raise standards through improving teaching has highlighted continuous professional development as one of the most significant issues in education management currently. The Teacher Training Agency (TTA) put forward a model for continuous professional development linked to the career structure of teachers. The TTA advocated that *professional lifelong learning should become a requirement for all teachers* in order to drive up standards in schools. Reflecting the changes through government decree of the last decade, the model preferred by the TTA focused more on the requirements of the school and *de facto*, less on the professional development needs of the individual teacher.

This was a radical shift of emphasis from the models of professional development prominent in the 1970s and 1980s when the needs of the teacher were seen as paramount. This shift was not considered to be problematic yet there are indications to the contrary. For instance, there is concern that despite generous funding in recent years progress in raising standards has been slower than expected. Why might this be? One reason might be the kind of training provided for teachers.

The Teacher Training Agency licensed teacher training to ensure that the needs of pupils, 'for too long ignored', were being met. All standards in TTA programmes were to be based on a technical-competency model and subjected to systematic evaluation. This would appear to be a reasonable way to ensure that training is effective and efficient but in actual fact there has been little research into what comprises effective professional development. For instance, researchers such as Potts (1998) criticise the technical competency-based approach to professional development because it neglects the social experience of teaching and learning which she sees as of paramount importance.

Certainly teachers have complained to us that their expectations from professional development courses have not always been met. Often this was because the specific contexts in which they were working were not taken sufficiently into account. Such things as the school culture, the catchment area, facilities and resources within the school can make all the difference as to what teachers are able to do. In themselves these factors neither make it possible nor impossible to get things done but they are integral aspects of the social experience of teaching and learning and as such need to be addressed in order to facilitate change.

The school effectiveness movement has become increasingly frustrated because, it seems, teachers do not readily make use of the instructional techniques for teaching which have been shown to be effective. Reynolds (1998) asks why teachers do not do what they are told to do. But if teachers do not see the relevance of these instructional techniques to their preferred way of teaching, why should they adopt them? Indeed, can they do so? Is it possible to teach effectively if you are being asked to work in a way that is foreign to you? If the method really goes against the grain of what you believe teaching and learning is all about, can you make use of it?

Or maybe it is that the teachers cannot see the techniques working with a particular group of pupils, or in a specific setting; after all, no single technique works in all situations (Clark 1993, 1996a). For sure there are numerous possible reasons why teaching is not as simple as implementing particular techniques.

☞ **Teaching is both a highly personal and individual experience.**

So much so that many learners may well recall the characteristics and personalities of their teachers rather than the subjects they taught. Ultimately teachers do things in their own way, they work idiosyncratically and manage to individualise prescriptive teaching programmes. The National Curriculum itself is a case in point.

This highly developed sense of individuality which teachers need to acquire if they are to teach, and especially if they are to teach well, is something that over the years has not been sufficiently recognised. Teachers were described by researchers until relatively recently as shadowy figures on the landscape, an amorphous group, almost as if they were incidental to the teaching and learning process. This needs to change if educational progress is to occur because as Fullan (1991) says there is no educational development without teacher development. It might also be prudent to provide a variety of professional development experiences to accommodate individual needs. While the aims and objectives on all courses could remain the same, the type of professional development process might well vary from course to course.

Some courses could be more teacher-centred and emanate principally from the interests and needs of the teachers themselves, making use of processes chosen and managed by teachers. Others could be school-centred and prescriptive. All, however, could be competency-based; the issue would be which competencies should be included, who decides on the competencies and how they should be taught. It would be interesting to compare and contrast through systematic monitoring and evaluation the outcomes of the different types of courses for effectiveness and efficiency.

My work indicates that courses that are teacher-focused – most of which used an integrated model of professional development – are perceived by teachers as being positive and useful experiences (Clark 1993). We think this approach is worth considering in greater detail.

The history of the development of the integrated model

This eclectic developmental model is based on the work of Hargreaves and Fullan (1992) which stated that the type of professional development most likely to facilitate ecological change, that is change in the workplace, was one that put the needs of the school first.

It emphasised the importance of taking into account the context of the working environment – in other words the day-to-day happenings in the classroom and the school. But Hargreaves and Fullan also described two other types of professional development which were desirable. We would suggest, from our work, that they were not only desirable, but essential, if real progress is to be made and teacher development is to occur. They are:

- teacher development as knowledge and skills development so that pupils can have improved opportunities to learn;
- teacher development as self-understanding where the focus is on the teacher as a person.

Gaunt (1997) suggests, and we would agree, that the *best* professional development ideally encompasses *all three types*. The *integrated model of professional development* attempts to incorporate all three types and in doing so aims to facilitate changes in teacher thinking and practice which can be observed in classrooms.

We know what characteristics, abilities and skills are required in order to teach gifted and talented pupils well. In other words, we know what kinds of change in thinking and practice are required to make a difference for the better in teaching and learning.

For instance, my own work (Clark 1996a, 1997) has shown that:

☞ **teachers who are successful with more able pupils have an extensive knowledge base about ways of working with them. They are creative teachers who facilitate creative responses in their pupils.**

When teaching they were prepared to take risks, to consider alternatives, to tolerate ambiguities, to encourage task commitment by giving learners more time to go into a project in depth, and were flexible in terms of finding ways forward. (Clark 1997)

The challenge, which is worldwide, is to train teachers who can work with gifted pupils in ways that are sufficiently sensitive, flexible, creative and skilled.

It is generally agreed that gifted and talented pupils require a great deal from their teachers. They prefer to be taught by teachers who:

- know their subject well
- are enthusiastic
- have a sense of humour
- are confident
- they can relate to
- are as much process-orientated in their teaching as product-orientated.

They are teachers who can facilitate learning in a creative learning environment (Clark 1995, Clark and Callow 1998, Clark and Shore 1998).

We suggest that looking at professional development from a different viewpoint might help teachers to rise to these challenges. In particular a collaborative and integrated approach to professional development looks as if it would be useful, making it possible for teachers to develop those characteristics listed above.

The integrated model is similar to that of Hargreaves and Fullan and includes Gaunt's three types of professional development. Its underlying aim is to influence thinking in order to change practice through:

- knowledge and skills development
- self-understanding
- ecological change.

Such a humanistic, integrated approach to the continuing professional development of teachers of gifted pupils appears to help them to provide appropriately challenging educational experiences *not least* because they themselves have had experience of learning in similar stimulating environments during the professional development experiences (Clark 1997, Clark and Callow 1998).

This model incorporates both the cognitive and affective domains of teaching and works with the whole person to achieve observed change in both thinking and practice.

Searching out such a model of professional development which helps teachers to improve their teaching has been at the heart of the inservice work we have undertaken in schools, for local education authorities and at universities over many years. We would not claim that this model works for all teachers, no one model could be expected to do this, but if offered as an alternative to the technical-competency model then we believe it can play an important part in the professional development of teachers of gifted and talented pupils.

An integrated model of professional development for teachers of gifted and talented pupils

The emergence of the model

This model of professional development:

- is the kind of professional development that aims to encourage perspective transformation and results in changing the thinking and practice of teachers (Diamond 1991);
- is a holistic development process in which teachers are emotionally as well as intellectually involved;
- makes a positive difference to their teaching;
- alters how they teach gifted pupils.
  (Clark 1996b)

This approach encourages teachers to understand what Schon (1987) describes as their 'knowledge in action', that is knowledge that can be observed when they act.

It is well known that teacher knowledge which influences everything they do in classrooms is most often 'taken-for-granted'. Teachers in busy classrooms do not have the time to reflect on everything they do but they need to be encouraged and given time to reflect on certain aspects of their practice at the very least. It is an important first step in beginning to understand what they are thinking and what they are doing.

In earlier work with Easen (1993), Clark discussed the importance of unveiling teacher conceptualisations of learning and the necessity for techniques to be used in professional development which encouraged teachers interested in special educational needs to investigate the 'taken-for-granted'. Later work investigated whether understanding the 'taken-for-granted' was also useful for teachers of bright pupils and whether it provided insight into how they taught gifted pupils.

Traditionally, such teacher knowledge has not been much investigated because it has not been valued by educational researchers. It has been considered to be largely anecdotal, context-bound and highly personal but work by Nias and Groundwater Smith (1988) and Cortazzi (1993) considers these aspects to be the very essence of what knowledge is and as such something to be explored, valued and developed. Nias describes knowledge as intensely personal but also morally purposeful and not something that may be transmitted through 'technically controlled conduits'.

Research done by Clark makes use of the personal and practical knowledge of teachers based on the hypothesis that it is a legitimate knowledge for research and a straightforward way to access the theory which influences their thinking and actions (Clark 1992a). Groundwater Smith (*ibid.*) sees the ultimate form as knowledge that is emancipatory-cognitive involving intersubjectivity, self-reflection and reflexivity. It is these processes that are used in the integrated model of professional development to help teachers make sense of their experiences.

There are many different types of knowledge, none of which, Clough and Barton (1998) maintain, is necessarily better than another. Nevertheless, in academia, as Gitlin, Bringhurst, Burns, Cooley, Myers, Price, Russell and Tiess (1992) comment, legitimate knowledge has been, and indeed by some positivists still is, considered to be knowledge that is theoretically objective, systematic and disinterested.

But all knowledge is subjective, unsystematic and biased to some extent. Knowledge is, *de facto*, partial and incomplete because it is always personal and reflects the ideas, thoughts, beliefs and assumptions of those who produce it (Clough and Barton 1998). Furthermore it is never complete because it is dynamic and changes through time and experience (Kuhn 1970). The integrated model of professional development takes this thinking into account and encourages teachers to question all types of knowledge and use it to increase their understanding of themselves and their world.

The main substance of this model is the use of the processes of intersubjectivity, self-reflection and reflexivity to move teachers through the three levels of knowledge described by Habermas (1976):

- the first level is technical-cognitive knowledge to be found in competency models of training;
- the second is practical knowledge which focuses attention almost entirely on classroom practice not taking into account any outside influences;
- the third is emancipatory knowledge. At the third level the teachers engage with the biggest questions of a social, political and economic nature which greatly influence the educational context, not least the classrooms in which they teach.

The integrated approach to professional development places great emphasis on the explication of teacher knowledge through two constructs:

- teachers' theory in action;
- the notion of the partiality and incompleteness of knowledge.

Three issues emerged as a result of working with teachers while using this approach:

- Reflexivity
- Notions of legitimate knowledge
- The development of 'authentic relationships'.

These issues, when elaborated, analysed and then synthesised, later provided a framework for this model of professional development which seems to enable teachers of gifted children to begin to 'reinvent' themselves in order to provide their pupils with an appropriate and challenging education.

The implementation of the model of integrated development

Reflexivity

As stated in *Towards Inclusive Schools?* (Clark, Dyson and Millward 1995) reflexivity is about testing assumptions, advocating, resisting and reconstructing resolutions. It is described by Winter (1989) as 'the process of bending back into one's subjective system of meanings'. It is about asking the question why and when one has received an answer again asking but why is that so? It also involves asking the ultimate question: if someone else were collecting this data would they collect it in the same way and would they interpret it in the same way? We construe reflexivity as a never-ending process of questioning interpretations, understandings and 'conclusions'. We see reflexivity as a crucial element in understanding what is implicit in both thinking and practice. It helps to make explicit what is implicit.

Findings from Clark suggest that:

☞ **reflexivity appears to stimulate thinking about alternative ways of behaving and thinking and thus provides the individual with greater impetus to change. It is important therefore in professional development situations to ensure that there is time to think reflexively about one's practice.**

In Clark (1997) *reflexivity stimulated by classroom observation* emerged as an important way forward. Observation is therefore a key technique in the model of integrated development as it provides opportunities for teachers to understand more fully what is going on in their classrooms.

The findings of this research confirmed the work of others (Tuttle and Becker 1980, Story 1985, Silver and Hanson 1988, and Whitlock and Ducette 1989 that successful teachers of more able learners:

- formed positive relationships with their pupils;
- provided quality and quantity of verbal interaction such that higher order thinking was routinely and actively encouraged;
- held creative productivity as their ultimate goal;
- displayed 'gifted behaviours' in their many personal and professional activities.

The reflexive process helped the teachers in this study to engage in depth with these issues.

The reflexive approach to data interpretation practised throughout this study resulted in these teachers and the course director:

- questioning the 'taken-for-granted';
- looking at things in different ways and searching for alternatives;
- challenging stereotypes;
- seeing things from different perspectives.

This two-year project:

- identified ways in which teachers and schools could improve their standards by differentiating the curriculum for more able pupils;
- provided research data on the basis of which such developments might be premised;
- encouraged teachers and schools to undertake classroom-based research;
- extended the range of the professional skills of teachers to include the teacher as researcher;
- helped the teachers to understand some of the complexities and subtleties of the professional development process through action research which resulted in observable change in classroom and school practice for more able and talented children.

All these outcomes provided the teachers and their schools with an *extensive knowledge base* to inform their work with gifted pupils.

Furthermore the usefulness of reflexivity as a teaching technique for gifted pupils was demonstrated in the paper 'Teaching Thinking Skills to Able Learners' (Clark 1995) a case study report describing the work of a middle school teacher who used *reflexive questioning* to challenge her more able pupils.

The paper developed Clark's work on reflexivity through the use of *dialectical dialogues*. These dialogues are necessary for the most rigorous analysis of data collected through 'action research'. They use a more structured type of reflexivity. The research question was whether this process could facilitate creative thinking and practice in the classroom. Having undertaken action research projects in their classrooms and schools, the group discussed their findings as a research community.

The findings of each researcher were interpreted collectively by the group who were actively encouraged to engage in a rigorous level of non-judgemental critique. The obvious became evident: group members often saw things very differently.

By asking questions like 'Is that the only way to look at that, what about turning that statement completely around?' or 'What about thinking about it from the opposite viewpoint . . .?' the teachers were required to consider possibilities which were diametrically opposed to their original interpretation.

This dialectical process promoted reflexivity and elicited deeper and broader questioning not only about the role of the teacher but also about that of the local education authority and the Government.

This research focused on whether the research community could act as a socially facilitating environment for the teachers. There is evidence to suggest, as Csikszentmihalyi, Rathunde and Whalen (1993) and George (1992, 1995) have shown, that socially facilitating environments are an important factor in initiating creative responses.

In addition, it considered whether this experience would encourage the teachers to provide socially facilitating environments for their gifted pupils. There was some evidence to suggest that following this professional development experience these teachers were creative in their responses to their pupils in general but especially to their more able pupils.

Legitimate knowledge

Bassey (1995: 3) describes knowledge as:

> Understandings about events and things and processes: it includes descriptions, explanations, value orientations, as well as knowledge of how these can be arrived at; in other words it includes knowledge that something is the case and knowledge about how to do something; it includes theory-in-literature as well as the personal theory of individuals which has not been articulated in writing.

By explicitly mentioning the personal theory of individuals, this comprehensive definition of knowledge does not follow the more conventional belief that knowledge is theory and therefore solely the domain of experts. Personal knowledge such as teachers' knowledge, based as it is on practical knowledge, is often undervalued because of such narrow notions.

But Gitlin (1992) argues that it is essential not to privilege one form of knowledge over another. He stresses the importance of always being prepared to question everything because all knowledge is partial and incomplete.

In Clark and Callow (1998) we argue, not for the first time, that it is essential that teachers explicate this practical knowledge as a first step towards a better understanding of themselves, their pupils, their schools and the education system. As part of this process they ask questions about everything they are considering.

This work (*ibid.*) suggests that if such questioning happens it appears to facilitate professional development often through interconnectivity. For instance, in 'A model of professional self-development for teachers working with more able pupils' (Clark 1996b) a combination of narrative and action research was used for this purpose. What this holistic and integrative process did was to intersect the personal and professional aspects of the teachers' lives and interconnect the micro world of each classroom with the macro world of the school and beyond.

Once teachers are au fait with the processes involved in this dynamic model for self-development, it is possible for individual teachers, even those working in unsupportive schools, to use narrative as a tool for self-development (Clark 1992a).

The development of 'Authentic relationships'

The preceding sections on '**reflexivity**' and '**legitimate knowledge**', together with this one on '**authentic relationships**' make the case for a new form of professional development which:

- emanates from the interests and needs of professionals as defined by themselves;
- works through processes which are largely chosen and managed by them;
- as its ultimate aim helps professionals to understand the world and take action.

Continuous professional development which seeks to be emancipatory in this way has some specific problems. Like emancipatory research it is part of a wider social process and is characterised by the exercise of power and the workings of vested interest. For example, it can serve to enhance the influence of professional developers and their careers. Dyson (1998) writes that the role of the professional intellectual, in this instance the professional developer, is questionable.

Issues concerning their motives, values, assumptions and beliefs require consideration. He believes that it is necessary for professional developers themselves to be reflexive in order to establish 'authentic' relationships with their clients but questions how far this is possible or desirable because of the expectations of clients. Research done by Clark illustrates firstly how this can be done and, secondly, the extent to which it is possible to create 'authentic relationships'.

'Teacher-Centred Development: A Way of Helping Able and Talented Students to Achieve' (Clark 1992b) describes how focusing on teachers' hopes, fears and concerns helps them to teach their more able and talented students with greater confidence. Teacher-Centred Development (TCD) was, and remains, useful for many reasons, but one of the most important is its ability to change perceptions. Describing and analysing positive experiences as well as negative experiences is possibly the most essential element in Teacher-Centred Development. Non-judgemental discussions are another fundamental element which build confidence. The agenda on TCD courses arises out of the general discussion and is in some ways set by the teachers. The role of the group leader is therefore different from the conventional role of knowledge disseminator.

It includes knowledge dissemination but it goes beyond this.

☛ **The role of the group leader is essentially catalytic.**

It is because of this that the process of continuing professional development can be restructured. Many of the conventional boundaries are broken down and power is more equally shared.

In practice this means that the roles of all who participate are reinvented. It results in an emancipatory experience for all. Lather (1990: 6) describes emancipatory research as a process which 'can lead to a pathway of a different truth'. We consider that this type of professional development – which was subsequently substantially built on in the model of integrated development – at best does the same because it questions current and favoured hegemonies and puts forward alternative possibilities.

As demonstrated above a dialogue between all aspects of the enquiry, debate, discussion or development is necessary in order to make this happen and one way to build such 'authentic relationships' is to work not only within the cognitive domain but also the affective domain of development. In other words what teachers feel most concerned about is seen as the priority for professional development. In 1995 in the report for the Department for Education and Employment, *Innovatory Practice in Mainstream Schools for Special Educational Needs*, Clark, Dyson, Millward and Skidmore found evidence that schools that considered themselves to be innovatory spent time focusing on the day-to-day concerns of their teachers through classroom-based research.

It is worth noting that in these schools teacher concerns were not seen as a sign of professional incompetence but rather of professional competence. The relationship between the management and the staff in these schools was 'authentic' in that the usual hierarchical boundaries did not operate in the classroom-based research activities, both were united in a common aim based on a consensus of opinion in order to find a way forward.

In the article 'Changing Teachers Through Telling Stories' (Clark 1993), it is the consensus of opinion between the teacher educator and the teachers about professional development and the professional development process that is the basis for working towards change. This paper describes reflexive reflection as well as constructivist approaches to learning in which the group leader acts as scaffolder providing a foothold or step to the next stage or point of learning.

Combined with reflexivity which enables the individual to question the 'taken-for-granted' and the idea that all knowledge is legitimate knowledge, the development of 'authentic' relationships is the engine which powers the emancipatory process of integrated professional development. Integrated development should result in the reconstruction of thinking and practice and in *Educating Able Children: Resource Issues and Processes for Teachers* (Clark and Callow 1998) a synthesis of this process was included together with suggestions of ways in which it could be further developed.

The following ideas were put forward:

- both able pupils and their teachers are resources to themselves, each other and their peers and should be actively encouraged to be so;
- both teachers and able pupils in particular – but all pupils – should be actively involved in school planning;
- observation should be used as a research tool to underpin effective action;
- planning and professional development need to be interlinked;
- the emphasis ought to be on the teacher-as-asset approach to professional development.

In *Educating Students with High Ability* (Clark and Shore 1998), a book written for a worldwide audience from widely differing cultural and educational backgrounds, an attempt was made to answer the most common questions asked by teachers of gifted students across the world. Day-to-day practice was viewed as the baseline for professional development facilitated through the integrated professional development process. Integrated professional development is the type of professional development which is within the realms of possibility for teachers in all contexts.

Conclusion

The essence of this chapter is that gifted pupils have the right to an appropriate education. They require a challenging and stimulating education and therefore they need to be educated by teachers who are highly skilled and confident.

The technical-competency model of professional development currently favoured which emphasises technical skills, we have argued, appears to have its limitations. At worst it can undermine and deskill teachers because it is based on the assumption that teachers do not already possess skills and competences. Little attempt is made to build on the skills that teachers already have. The integrated model sets out to make explicit use of what teachers have to offer. It is fundamentally emancipatory in nature.

We have suggested that the integrated model of professional development which focuses on both the intellectual as well as the affective domains of learning can begin to reconstruct the thinking and practice of teachers of gifted and talented pupils. It is a model that has applicability in all educational contexts to a greater or lesser extent depending on the political and cultural agenda.

The needs of gifted and talented pupils and their teachers have been neglected in the past. But they are now firmly on the political agenda as part of the school improvement and raising standards initiative. Their rights are at last being considered. What is also required is a radical revision of teacher professional development to enhance competency, instil confidence and make certain that the abilities of gifted and talented pupils are fully developed by their teachers.

This book is about making the most of available resources to improve the education of gifted and talented pupils. Clearly teachers are one of the main resources. It is therefore important to find out which of the current approaches to professional development teachers find most helpful. Equally it is necessary to evolve innovative approaches which will benefit teachers even more. In the chapter that follows we describe a number of possible ways forward.

References

Bassey, M. (1995) *Creating Education Through Research*. Newark: Kirklington Moor Press.

Clark, C. (1992a) 'Diary Writing and Analysis: an emancipatory tool for teachers in training', a paper prepared for the British Educational Research Association Annual Conference, Stirling.

Clark, C. (1992b) 'Teacher-Centred Development: A Way of Helping Able and Talented Students to Achieve', in Conference Papers of the 1992 National Association for Able Children in Education and the National Association for Gifted Children International Conference, Oxford. Middlesex: Middlesex University.

Clark, C. (1993) 'Changing Teachers Through Telling Stories', *Support for Learning* **8**(1), 31–4.

Clark, C. (1995) 'Teaching Thinking Skills to Able Learners', *Flying High*, Spring, 6–9.

Clark, C. (1996a) *More Able and Talented Pupils: Developing Practice in Cleveland Primary and Secondary Schools*. Cleveland: Cleveland LEA.

Clark, C. (1996b) 'A model of professional self-development for teachers working with more able pupils', in Tilsley, P. and Clark, C. (eds) Worcester Papers in Education, Autumn, **1**, 33–8.

Clark, C. (1997) 'Using Action Research to Foster a Creative Response to Teaching More Able Pupils', *High Ability Studies* **8**(1), 95–111.

Clark, C. (1999) 'Rethinking the Issue of the Professional Development of Teachers of Able Pupils', *Educating Able Children* **3**, Spring, 22–8.

Clark, C. and Callow, R. (1998) *Educating Able Children: Resource Issues and Processes for Teachers*. London: David Fulton Publishers.

Clark, C., Dyson, A. and Millward, A. J. (eds) (1995) *Towards Inclusive Schools?* London: David Fulton Publishers.

Clark, C., Dyson, A., Millward, A. J. and Skidmore, D. (1995) *Innovatory Practice in Mainstream Schools for Special Educational Needs*. London: The Stationery Office.

Clark, C. and Easen, P. (1993) 'Turning the Kaleidoscope: Working with teachers concerned about special educational needs', in Dyson, A. and Gains, C. (eds) *Rethinking Special Educational Needs in Mainstream Schools: Towards the Year 2000*. London: David Fulton Publishers.

Clark, C. and Shore, B. (1998) *Educating Students with High Ability*. Paris: United Nations Education and Science Organisation (UNESCO).

Clough, P. and Barton, L. (eds) (1998) *Articulating with Difficulty*. London: Paul

Chapman Publishing.

Cortazzi, M. (1993) *Narrative Analysis.* London: Falmer Press.

Csikszentmihalyi, M., Rathunde, K. and Whalen, S. (1993) *Talented Teenagers: the roots of success and failure.* Cambridge: Cambridge University Press.

Department for Education and Employment (DfEE) (1997) *Excellence in Schools.* London: The Stationery Office.

Diamond, C. T. P. (1991) *Teacher Education as Transformation.* Buckingham: Open University Press.

Dyson, A. (1998) 'Professional Intellectuals from Powerful Groups: wrong from the start?', in Clough, P. and Barton, L. (eds) *Articulating with Difficulty.* London: Paul Chapman Publishing.

Fullan, M. (1991) *The New Meaning of Educational Change* (2nd edn). London: Cassell.

Gaunt, D. (1997) 'Building on the Past: New Opportunities for the Profession', in Tomlinson, H. (ed.) *Managing Continuing Professional Development in Schools.* London: Paul Chapman Publishing.

George, D. (1992) *The Challenge of the Able Child.* London: David Fulton Publishers.

George, D. (1995) *Gifted Education: identification and provision.* London: David Fulton Publishers.

Gitlin, A., Bringhurst, K., Burns, M., Cooley, V., Myers, B., Price, K., Russell, R. and Tiess, P. (1992) *Teachers' Voices for School Change.* London: Routledge.

Habermas, J. (1976) *Communication and the Evolution of Society.* London: Falmer Press.

Hackett, G. (1998) 'Coasting Schools Targeted', *Times Educational Supplement,* 13 November.

Hargreaves, A. and Fullan, M. G. (eds) (1992) *Understanding Teacher Development.* London: Cassell.

Her Majesty's Inspectorate (HMI) (1992) *The Education of Very Able Children in Maintained Schools.* London: HMSO.

Kuhn, T. (1970) *The Structure of Scientific Revolutions.* Chicago: University of Chicago Press.

Lather, P. (1990) 'Reinscribing otherwise: the play of values in the practices of human sciences', in Guba, E. G. (ed.) *The Paradigm Dialog.* London: Sage.

Nias, J. and Groundwater Smith, S. (eds) (1988) *The Enquiring Teacher.* London: Falmer Press.

Potts, P. (1998) 'Knowledge is not enough: an exploration of what we can expect from enquiries which are social', in Clough, P. and Barton, L. (eds) *Articulating with Difficulty.* London: Paul Chapman Publishing.

Reynolds, D. (1998) 'The school effectiveness mission has only just begun', *Times Educational Supplement,* 20 February.

Schon, D. A. (1987) *Educating the Reflective Practitioner.* San Francisco: Jossey-Bass.

Silver, H. and Hanson, J. (1988) 'Research on Teaching Styles of Teachers of the

Gifted', *Roeper Review* **1**, 144–6.

Story, C. (1985) 'Facilitator of learning: a microethnic study of the teacher of the gifted', *Gifted Education Quarterly* **29**,155–9.

Tuttle, G. B. and Becker, L. A. (1980) *Program Design and Development for Gifted and Talented Students.* Washington DC: National Education Association.

Whitlock, M. and Ducette, J. (1989) 'Outstanding and average teachers of the gifted', *Gifted Education Quarterly* **33**, 15–21.

Winter, R. (1989) *Learning from Experience.* Lewes: Falmer Press.

CHAPTER 4

Integrated professional development as a resource for teachers of gifted and talented pupils

Some underlying key issues

1. Teaching gifted and talented children is a challenge

In order to accrue the maximum benefit from their schooling, gifted and talented pupils often make exceptional demands on their teachers. Most of these pupils have an inexhaustible supply of concentration, enthusiasm and ability which, although uplifting for teachers, can also be problematic for teachers with whole-class responsibilities: these responsibilities require the teacher to give all pupils their fair share of teacher time and attention.

In most classes there is a wide range of ability and in mixed-ability classes there is an even greater range of ability. Teachers therefore have their work cut out if they are to differentiate the curriculum appropriately for all pupils.

We know that gifted and talented pupils thrive on exceptional learning experiences (Freeman 1998). But they are not alone; most pupils do. This is why all pupils are entitled to receive teaching that is challenging, exciting and meaningful. Gifted and talented pupils, however, have a thirst for knowledge and understanding which marks them out from the rest.

It appears to be *essential* for them to learn by investigating in greater breadth and depth and at a faster pace than their peers. If they are not stimulated by their experiences then gifted and talented pupils may well become alienated from school. Teachers are, without doubt, one of the most important resources available to ensure that this does not happen. They are responsible for planning and managing learning experiences. They also very importantly mediate learning. It is the *quality* of that mediation which differentiates the satisfactory learning experience from the exceptional.

Teachers should have among other things:

- easy access to advice about planning, managing and mediating the learning of gifted and talented pupils;
- knowledge of identification techniques;

- ways of monitoring progress and evaluating learning experiences.

Generally this is acquired through professional development. In our view the context within which professional development takes place requires careful consideration. If it is not perceived as meaningful and purposive by teachers then it is a waste of time, effort and money. We believe that what appears to make a difference is whether what is offered focuses on the personal as well as the professional aspects of the topic under discussion, in other words, if an integrated approach to professional development is used.

2. Why professional development may not happen

Before we consider how to provide effective professional development, it is vital to discuss what might be the first step taken by a teacher who wishes to find out more about teaching gifted and talented pupils.

☞ **The initial response to a teacher's request for support and advice from the head teacher, head of department or whichever member of the management team is involved, is crucially important.**

The teacher might well say something like, 'I have a particularly bright group of children in the top set this year and within that there are several high-fliers who are outstanding. I need some help, please.'

The reply given is tremendously important; so much depends on that rejoinder. Of course, the teacher may not have chosen the best moment to approach his or her colleague but nevertheless there are ways and ways of responding. There are also a variety of different ways of indicating that this is an issue that requires, and will get, consideration and action.

It is often at this crucial, tentative stage in the professional development process that things can go wrong because teachers feel unsupported if they do not get what they construe to be a positive response to their request. This can result in them retreating back into their classrooms feeling frustrated and even alienated. Sometimes teachers retreat to their classrooms and do not put their heads above the parapet again. This tends to happen in schools that do not put teachers first. In these schools either nothing is done to help or the teacher is left with a feeling of professional incompetence because she/he has asked for help. Some teachers have reported to us that if their request does not link into the professional development programme already arranged by the senior management team then there is little chance that their cry for help will be heeded.

Parents, school governors, senior teachers, head teachers and educational administrators as well as Ofsted inspectors and politicians need to think again if this is the likely response to a *cri de coeur* from a class teacher.

☞ **Some degree of flexibility to deal with spontaneous requests from class and subject teachers should be inbuilt into inservice programmes.**

Circumstances in schools can change quite dramatically and suddenly, for instance, with a new intake of pupils. Sometimes it is not efficacious to wait another academic year before slotting an issue into the professional development programme when there is a strong feeling among staff that something needs to be done now.

3. *The necessity for teaching to be regarded as a complex activity*

☞ **A negative response to a teacher's request for help can indicate a lack of real understanding about what it is, on a daily basis, that teachers do.**

Why it is that some senior teachers, who themselves were once class and subject teachers, appear to be unable to remember the complexity of classroom life is a mystery. But it is sometimes the case.

First, there is the tangled web of relationships within a class of 30 individuals which in itself makes teaching complicated enough. But also there are additional layers of subtleties, nuances and ambiguities about what is said and done during teaching and learning that have to be taken into account if effective teaching and learning is to occur.

Senior managers and school governors in some schools and advisers and inspectors in local education authorities appear to have forgotten this. Is this because they are entirely focused on meeting their own targets and objectives?

It has been said before, but it is perhaps worth saying again, that at no other time in our lives are we expected to relate constantly to 30 other people in such intimate circumstances, and over such a long period of time, as when we are in school. In school, pupils are obliged to live and work cheek by jowl with peers who, in other circumstances, they might not choose to be with because they have little in common with them. This may not necessarily be a bad thing but it can, and does, create demands on pupils and also, most particularly, on teachers. Other factors including the backgrounds of pupils, their abilities and aptitudes also have to be taken into account by the teacher who wants to teach well.

It is important to add that such diversity can add much that is positive to the teaching and learning experience. But it is not always easy to utilise all that pupils have to offer within National Curriculum timetables where time is of the essence. However, it is teachers who, rightly, have to ensure that diverse groups of pupils – irrespective of culture, class, religion or ability – are well taught.

Successful teaching is a combination of a multiplicity of high level skills, knowledge, intense motivation and intuition. It is a complicated business. Speaking in generalities about good teaching and providing four or five examples of what good teaching comprises – typically the response in government documentation – however well-meaning, is therefore insufficient. The time has come to look again in far more detail at what is involved in teaching and learning in specific circumstances. By doing so the art and the science of teaching ought to be better understood.

In the last few years more research – for instance, that sponsored by the Government through the Education and Social Research Council – has focused, not before time, on the processes of teaching and learning in classrooms. When the work of teachers is better understood by teachers, educationalists and the public at large, hopefully they will get a better press and teacher morale will rise. Not only this but the professional development of teachers might well be seen in a different light.

Any request for professional development that is situation-specific and relates directly to classroom teaching will be seen as a sign of professional competence rather than the opposite, as it so often is at present.

Teachers are first and foremost human beings, despite claims by some to the contrary. Like any other professionals they thrive on personal and professional satisfaction.

☞ **One of the basic differences between good and poor schools appears to be whether or not continual, explicit acknowledgement is made of the efforts made by individual teachers.**

How many times have teachers said to us, 'I don't mind doing the extra at all, I just wish the Head would say thank you'?

4. Teachers need to feel, and be, valued by their schools

☞ **Those schools that value staff and show it are likely to be teacher-centred in much that they do.**

There are schools that take care of their teachers in the way that they hope the teachers will take care of their pupils.

Such schools are prepared to focus on issues such as the one we highlighted above starting from the baseline that, unless there is evidence to the contrary, a teacher is professionally competent with skills which require honing in order to meet the demands of the specific situation. The request is therefore not seen as one that denotes weakness and incompetence; in fact, it is believed to demonstrate the opposite of this.

5. Teachers need to have a say in the content and processes of the professional development experience

The model of professional development upon which this book focuses arises specifically from teacher-need in his or her own classroom setting. In this way the starting point for the process should be one of relevance to that particular teacher and one to which colleagues can also relate. By using this approach to professional development a basic difficulty with teacher development should already have been overcome. Time, effort and money should not have been wasted on providing something which is seen, whether in actuality it is so or not, as irrelevant by the teachers for whom it is intended.

We should stress that this approach does not mean that issues beyond the classroom are not discussed. The starting point is a particular classroom or a specific pupil but from the work we have done the end point often goes far beyond that. The microcosm of education in the classroom leads to the exploration of the broader context, the macrocosm. So, for instance, a teacher who wants to know about the best ways of teaching her brightest pupil may well look at how learning occurs and get into learning theory in order to find the answer.

Some examples of how an integrated approach to professional development might work in practice

1. Using teacher concerns to lead professional development

EXAMPLE 1: THE HISTORY DEPARTMENT SEMINAR

Presenting problem – how to ensure that gifted and talented pupils are 'stretched' in history lessons.

Interested teachers – the History Department

Mode – seminar

Focus – volunteers present brief case studies of examples of their practice that appeared to help gifted and talented pupils. This is followed by discussion in order to clarify aspects of particular interest or importance which may be of use to colleagues.

Outcome – head of department or nominated colleague to ensure each member of the team has briefing paper with seminar outcomes.

The requesting teacher should hopefully leave the seminar with more ideas than he/she came with. If this did not happen because no ideas were forthcoming then this in itself is a useful starting point. A member of the team needs to contact the specialist teacher for gifted and talented either in the school or within the local education authority (through the appropriate channels) to ask for help and advice.

Then several things might happen, for instance:

- Members of the department could take chapters of book(s) recommended by colleagues or the specialist teacher as useful and at the next seminar they could present their analysis of the ideas they read about.
- They could try out materials, provided by colleagues or the specialist, and make a report about them to the group.
- They could ask the specialist to talk to them about ways of managing and organising learning so that gifted and talented pupils get a fairer deal.

In a few schools we have worked in, as the issues have got bigger and in some instances more generalisable, the original department involved has asked the staff as a whole if there would be sufficient interest to run a school-based course on the topic. For instance, following a seminar, such as we described above, the English department in one school systematically studied their questioning techniques. They were interested to find out which kinds of questions appeared to stimulate higher level responses from pupils, especially gifted and talented pupils. What they found out they eventually shared with other departments. This was in a school whose culture could be described as 'spontaneously collaborative', that is a school used to working in teams and across subject and key stage boundaries. The teachers were not pushed into mandatory collaboration, which Easen and Biott (1994) state creates as many tensions as it seeks to ameliorate.

The model develops in this way:

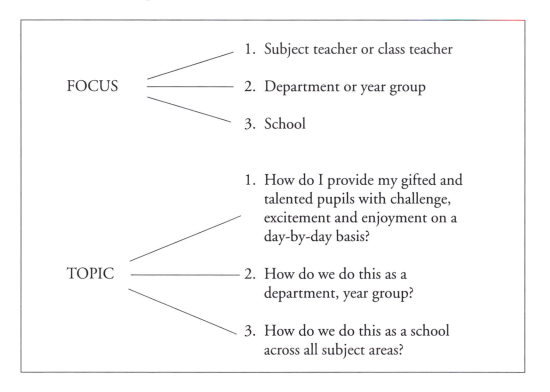

A key characteristic of this model is the involvement of the teachers from the beginning and throughout. Jordan (1994) comments that one-shot inputs on topics identified by managers have only limited impact on thinking and practice so this way of working, identified by teachers, is definitely worth considering.

The seeds for the growth of creative classrooms are sown, tended and brought to fruition by creative teachers. The question from a professional development viewpoint is how to nurture such creative teachers. Consultative collaboration is perhaps one way.

EXAMPLE 2: USING CONSULTATIVE COLLABORATION

As with the approach described above, this second example of integrated professional development has at its heart the aim of maximising the teacher resource available to gifted and talented pupils. These pupils in particular seem to benefit from being in creative classrooms (George 1992).

Such classrooms are managed positively: learners are encouraged to question, follow their own interests and produce unusual and unexpected work outcomes which are welcomed and valued.

Consultative collaboration is one way of enabling teachers to manage such classrooms. In our experience teachers often find it easier to learn from their peers than from authoritative colleagues who are senior to them or from experts without the school. Consultative collaboration gives teachers this opportunity.

This is not to say such people should never be involved in professional development, nor is it to say that they have nothing to offer, but it is important to be aware that their involvement can create 'them and us' barriers. What is always required is careful consideration of the role of course leader. Without this the teaching and learning process can become complicated to the extent that communication becomes problematic. Dilemmas about course content and other fundamental issues, for instance the vexed question of the relationship between theory and practice, can become heightened. Teachers in this kind of situation become resistant to 'new ideas' and 'different approaches'.

On courses we have run course members have prefaced statements with, 'Well, in theory that might be so but in my experience it is not possible.'

If time is not given to address these concerns democratically – that is by allowing views to be expressed and fully explained before they are further explored in an atmosphere which encourages all to have their say and where no one, not even the group leader, is acknowledged as knowing all the answers – then the process of professional development can grind to a halt. Ultimately these kinds of criticisms, if not dealt with, can result in questioning the efficacy of the professional development programme in terms of effectiveness and whether it is value for money.

What this comes down to is that teachers have to play a major part in their own professional development if it is to affect what they think and what they do in classrooms.

Reynolds (1998), focusing on ways of improving schools, stressed the fundamental need to discover how teachers can be influenced to work in different ways which appear to help pupils do well at school. Integrated approaches to professional development may well be a way forward.

> **Consultative collaboration, one kind of integrated development, obviates the need for a traditional leader role and for this reason alone appealed to a lot of teachers we have worked with.**

It also has resulted in a number of teachers who have used it to develop their teaching of gifted and talented pupils perceiving themselves as being more adventurous, confident and creative in their teaching. What is this approach and how does it work?

Consultative collaboration (timescale half an hour approximately)

The procedure

1. Teacher who has volunteered for this activity to provide a mini case history of the gifted and talented pupil causing concern (5 mins).
2. Teacher to outline what has already been done, indicating what helped the pupil and what did not help (5 mins).
3. Teacher shares ongoing concerns (5 mins).
4. From his/her own experience the consultant suggests ideas of ways forward (10 mins approximately).

The process

1. This is not an evaluation of the practice of the colleague. It is a non-judgemental activity.
2. The consultant should not criticise, even constructively, but can ask for clarification or more information.
3. If the consultant cannot think of where to go next, it is sensible to go to the literature for ideas or colleagues with more experience.

Although even one session like this can be helpful, consultative collaboration seems to work best when the two teachers meet together on a once per week or fortnight basis because this makes it possible to follow up on what has happened and develop things further. It is also helpful to transform consultative collaboration into reciprocal collaborative consultation so that the roles are reversed: one session you are a consultant and the next you are a consultee. By doing this, teachers report that they become less defensive becuase they are not seen to be the ones always asking for help, and also they begin to feel more skilled because they are actually getting the opportunity to use their experience to help their colleague.

Reciprocal collaboration

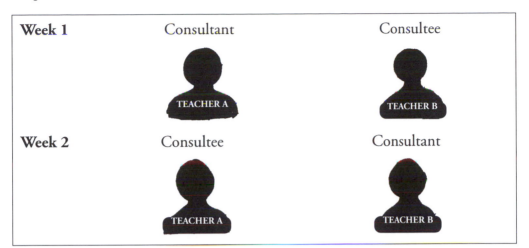

The next stage is for well-established dyads to go beyond their classroom and school and make use of the experience of other people. Some pairs decide to research the consultation topic by undertaking reading of recent literature on the topic or by attending courses so that they can share their extended knowledge and use it to inform their actions. The teachers who do this are generally those for whom the process of collaborative consultation is seen by the school as part of their ongoing professional development. In some schools these teachers have been asked to share this experience with other colleagues to encourage them to become involved.

There are many versions of this kind of sharing of experience and knowledge. A similar process is advocated by Hanko (1985): its aim is also to enhance the self-esteem of teachers, facilitate professional development and ultimately influence classroom practice.

School-wide consultative collaboration as part of professional development

Term 1	Consultation dyad of two colleagues, who are friends and volunteers, to work reciprocally using consultative collaboration on a once-weekly or fortnightly basis.
Term 2	This dyad splits and works with two other volunteer colleagues reciprocally on the same basis.
Term 3	If prepared, the four colleagues can share their experiences of working with this process with a larger group of staff, either at key stage, departmental or faculty level, or even to the whole school.
Term 4	More colleagues become involved in collaborative consultation, sharing outcomes school-wide with the aim of increasing the repertoire of teaching strategies for gifted and talented children within the school.

Consultative collaboration is based on a topic agreed by both teachers typically focusing on questions such as:

- How do I ensure that my brightest pupils make the best use of my time in maths lessons?
- How can I group my students in English lessons and plan appropriately so that the very brightest ones find the work stimulating?

It is *essential* that the teacher acting as consultant does not comment judgementally on the information provided by the consultee. We believe that educationalists have a real problem in *not* being judgemental. Time and again we have found that when groups of teachers are asked to watch a video of a colleague teaching in order to do a systematic analysis, there is a tendency to emphasise the negatives and omit the positives. The reason most often given by the teachers is that 'good practice' is expected of a competent teacher. However, in terms of personal and professional growth it is as necessary to be praised for what is going well as much as criticised for what is going wrong. Our concern, furthermore, is that the same hypercritical attitude is found in classrooms where good work outcomes and good behaviour are taken for granted and not commented upon whereas poor work and poor behaviour merit a great deal of attention. How might this affect gifted and talented pupils? And indeed all pupils?

What the consultant *is* expected to do in order to help the consultee develop his/her thinking and understanding of the topic is to affirm what can be affirmed along the lines of, 'Well, yes I've been in that kind of situation. . .' and talk about what he/she did. What the consultant says is not to be taken as *the answer* to the problem; it is simply a suggestion, a possibility. Following this there may be some agreement about what future action the consultee might like to take.

As the pair become more experienced in the process of reciprocal consultative collaboration, the scope of the consultation can be widened through:

- reading around the topic;
- the analysis and discussion of recently published research on the topic;
- attending courses at the university or LEA so that they can further extend their knowledge.

Over time it is also possible and, indeed likely, that the dyad will make use of more sophisticated questioning techniques and analytical comment which can result in deeper and even lateral thinking. This questioning remains non- judgemental but it is more challenging than during the earlier sessions. For instance:

'I wonder if that's the only way to look at what happened there, what if we look at it this way . . .?'
'How does that fit with what Freeman says about very bright girls?'
'Just take me step by step through what you said and what he said.'

This last type of comment is often useful in drawing attention to a point that was missed in the initial presentation.

EXAMPLE 3: PROFESSIONAL DEVELOPMENT BASED ON TEACHER PLANNING

Teacher planning can provide an insight into teacher thinking as well as practice.

As with the examples of integrated professional development already described, this is a teacher-centred and teacher-friendly process. It aims to deal not only with professional issues but also the personal aspects for teachers as individuals, in other words how teachers feel about what they are doing.

This approach seems to work well for professional development purposes if plans, including evaluations, for a series of consecutive lessons on a topic are analysed, ideally by the teacher and two colleagues with whom the teacher is confident (Figure 4.1). The idea is that by reading through and 'eyeballing' the data, each teacher picks out items of interest because they are usual, that is they occur often – or unusual because they occur only once. Or they might pick out something that they are not clear about but that seems interesting, or ask about an aspect which appears to have been omitted. In other words, they pick out what seems significant to them.

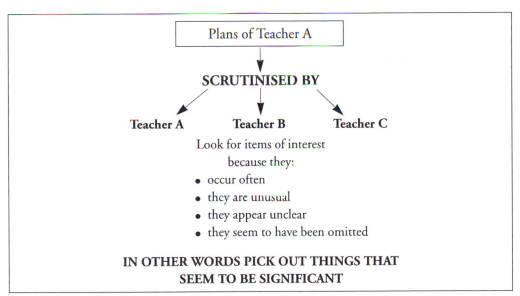

Figure 4.1 Professional development through focusing on teacher planning

The discussion, led by the teacher who made the plans, aims to clarify what was planned and what resulted from those plans. It will also raise additional matters which will be mentioned as the discussion unfolds about possible alternative ways of managing and organising learning, again as in collaborative consultation making use of the expertise and experience of all of the teachers. The reason why it is good to have three teachers working together rather than two, as stated earlier in this book, is that it makes for a more powerful analysis if three people agree on an interpretation rather than two. However, even if the three analysts disagree over their interpretation, the conversations can still be very useful from a professional viewpoint because they generate discussion. It is only if one person insists that they are right in their interpretation and the others are wrong that difficulties can occur. As with consultative collaboration, these discussion need to be non-judgemental, and decisions about what to do next and how to take on the next stage of professional development are up to the teacher whose lesson plans are being discussed, and not the analyst colleagues.

The timescale for this activity varies. It can be shortened on the day if each teacher has had time beforehand to read and annotate the plans, which means highlighting key points and noting down any queries for clarification. It also, of course, depends on the number of plans to be read. If it is four or five, then the discussion about the annotated plans can be less than 45 minutes, with about five minutes for the teacher to sum up her/his plan of action.

Where this approach is part of the school's professional development plan, it is possible for each member of the group to present plans in turn so that the process is equable. In this way in an academic year each teacher, if the group meets fortnightly, will get the chance to present a number of plans on different subjects. As with the strategy for professional development described above, subject to the willingness of the participants, there is no reason why this activity cannot be shared with other members of staff so that they can think about whether they would like to try it.

Another possibility for teachers who are interested in their mental planning, that is planning which they do in response to unexpected stimuli in the classroom setting – often sparked by pupils who say, 'Miss, can I do this instead because . . .?' – is to spend time systematically analysing these responses. Of course it does mean that some kind of account or professional diary has to be kept by the teacher, most often after the event, perhaps at the end of a day or week. It is also necessary for teachers to include in these accounts what was actually (or as near actually as possible) said and done, rather like a script, for them to be most useful. But for teachers who find it helpful to do this, and maybe cathartic because they use the diary to give vent to their feelings, this is a creative way to take things forward.

Diary-keeping can be a useful professional development activity: one which can be done alone if necessary. Work that I have done with student teachers, for instance, indicated that there were benefits, not least a feeling of relief because some negative feelings had been off-loaded, and they reported that they were able to view the pupil or the incident in a more professional light (Clark 1992). However, if the diary is shared or partly shared with a colleague, then some teachers report more positive outcomes, because, as one teacher put it, 'It felt to me that I was halving the problem.' But it would be incorrect to imagine that teachers only write about problems and concerns in these diaries. With encouragement the students in my study also wrote about what went well, and the discussion was about how these ideas and events might be exploited further. One caveat about diary sharing is that diaries to most people are private, and the idea of sharing what is private is not feasible. If diaries are to be shared it must be done with the permission of the writer and not made mandatory.

Making use of mental planning for professional development purposes

a) Note down instances in the classroom when it is necessary to respond to an unexpected stimulus – in a busy classroom there can be a number of these every day.

b) Keep some kind of account of daily happenings in the classroom, perhaps in the form of a diary.

In both instances include as near as possible scripts of the exchanges between those involved whether pupil/pupil(s) or teacher/pupil.

Systematically analyse the accounts. Ask yourself questions such as:

What was going on here?

Why did that happen?

Why did that not happen?

Are there any alternative explanations? What might they be?

How can what happened be capitalised on?

EXAMPLE 4: PROFESSIONAL DEVELOPMENT BASED ON OBSERVATION

Teacher research can include data collected among other ways through:

- classroom observation
- narrative

Observation data can also be used to provide data for consultative collaboration.

However used, in the integrated approach to professional development, observation data should be based on the process of:

- description
- clarification
- development or future action

It was suggested earlier that data from observation can be used for many purposes ranging from pupil assessment to helping to provide an appropriate curriculum for gifted and talented pupils. It can also be utilised, following the framework described above, for consultative collaboration purposes, either by pairs of teachers, teachers at a particular key stage, teachers who teach a certain subject or for the whole school for professional development. To use it most successfully at whatever leve, the process based on description, clarification and development must be adhered to. It is important to remember that any pupil observation says as much about the teacher as the pupil. It touches on how the lesson was organised, how the teacher managed the class and the pupil or pupils being observed, whether what the pupils required for the task was at hand, what the reactions of the pupils were and so on. Observation therefore exposes teachers and teaching as well as pupils and learning. Only if a process such as the one used in these examples is adopted is the danger of exposure to negative criticism averted. Constructive suggestions of alternative ways of working are permissible. When a teacher says, 'I think I've run out of ideas. I don't know what to do next. Any suggestions?', then is the time for partners to bring forward ideas from their experience and imagination. It is a confident teacher who is prepared to allow observation data to be discussed by the whole staff, but where the rules described above are adhered to it might become possible. When it is used as a stimulus for the whole staff, observation data can be a vehicle for the discussion of key issues about teaching and learning overall or about teaching different groups of pupils such as the gifted and talented.

EXAMPLE 5: PROFESSIONAL DEVELOPMENT BASED ON TEACHER RESEARCH

Teacher research can include data collected among other ways through:

- classroom observation
- narrative including anecdote
- planning
- diaries
- action research

Each of the examples of approaches to integrated professional development described earlier are types of teacher research. Collaborative consultation makes use of teacher narrative, including anecdotes, to collect data (Cotazzi 1993); the collaborative analysis of both teacher planning and classroom observation use data collection techniques which encourage the systematic deliberation of teaching and learning experiences. All encourage reflexivity, that is, the ability to perceive experiences in more than one way and accept that there is more than one interpretation of an action, a conversation or an interaction between teacher and pupil. Reflexibility encompasses, as Winter (1989) says, the willingness to keep on asking 'But why?' in response to every answer to a question, in a kind of quest for an ultimate truth which perhaps can never be found. Instead there is a point when people who ask the question agree for the moment to come to a consensus or hiatus and test their hypothesis in action before returning to the point at issue.

REFLEXIVITY IS THE KEY TO SYSTEMATIC ANALYSIS

In many ways these approaches interface with action research, the type of research teachers think of as most manageable and teacher-friendly (McNiff 1993). Purist action researchers consider that it neccessitates the researcher, having decided on the issue or problem to be tackled, to then do something which they describe and analyse to see if it achieves what they want to achieve. Whether the activities described in this chapter adhere to this model exactly is a point for discussion. But they certainly do encourage teachers to research their own classrooms by developing their understanding. There are good reasons for using these activities as well as action research in its more conventional form to further the development of individual teachers or schools because it is based on researching into issues considered by the teachers themselves to be of importance. To this end, like these other approaches, action research is a teacher-centred approach and unlikely to raise the hackles of teachers as some of the approaches appear to do which do not take teachers' views and experience into account.

The argument for teachers to engage in some type of teacher research activity is well made by the TTA who, in the late 1990s, put forward a pilot scheme for interested schools to become research communities. The progress of these schools and the resulting outcomes from the teacher research programme are being carefully monitored. Part of the value of this experience is that it will provide teachers with the possibility of coming to terms with the theory which underpins their practice. One meaning of the word 'theory' is the exposition of the principles which underlie a phenomenon; in other words, the explication of what often remains implicit when an activity, event or series of events occurs. Teaching and learning are such a series of events. Like any other activity, teaching cannot of its very nature be atheoretical, although it may be perceived as such by teachers. Many teachers would agree with the master's degree student who said, 'Oh, I don't work with theories, I'm too busy getting on with the job to theorise.' But in fact, in order to be able to function in the classroom it is necessary to theorise, even if it is not something the practitioner is aware of doing. Research done by Clandinin (1986), Louden (1991), Knowles (1992) and Clark (1993a) suggests that a teacher's theory is what he or she does in practice, and what is done in practice is influenced by values, beliefs and assumptions: in brief, life experience. So, as was stated previously, the planning a teacher does, the observations undertaken, the diaries kept as well as evaluations of lessons, inputs at staff meetings and outcomes from professional development days, all can provide information, if scrutinised systematically, about the theory which underpins a teacher's practice. Thus teachers who decide to research their own practice will be able to work from an evidence base as well as from intuition, common sense, expertise and, of course, experience: a formidable combination which cannot fail to influence and inform practice.

In conclusion, it has been argued here that professional development programmes which foster the holistic development of teachers enhance their ability to analyse their teaching experience and develop understandings of themselves, their pupils, their school as an institution and the education system in which they work. Without this it is difficult if not impossible to begin to meet the needs of individual pupils including gifted and talented pupils. This kind of analysis is necessary for precisely differentiated and individualised learning to happen, otherwise teachers have to revert to instinct and rule-of-thumb judgements. Often over time, instinct and heuristic responses become well-used skills and very useful, but when they are combined with evidence more systematically collected and analysed which is also stronger, the outcomes for pupils are that much more satisfactory because a lot of guesswork about where pupils are 'at', how much progress they are making in a lesson and what they are capable of is removed. In other words, teachers can act in a more professional manner because they can have greater confidence about why they are doing what they are doing in the way they are doing it.

Two opposing models of professional development

Teacher-deficit model	Teacher-as-asset model
1. Training imposed	1. Professional development experiences agreed by staff
2. Teachers' opinions about the programme not invited	2. Teachers invited to make suggestions for the programmes
3. Teachers told what they should be doing in class by programme leader	3. Using evidence from their classroom-based research, ways forward are formulated by staff
4. No recognition of what it is that teachers are already doing	4. Recognition of what teachers are already doing used as a starting point for future developments

Schools which value their teachers show that they do so by 'valuing in action', that is they not only say that they value staff but they do things to show that this is so. The teacher-as-asset description of professional development is an example of valuing in action. It enables schools to actualise the teacher resource to the full by providing professional development experiences that go beyond training and towards personal and professional education. As a result these teachers are better equipped to cope with change because they will have greater understanding of their thinking and practice. They will also be clearer about what they actually do when they are teaching and why they do it. This comes about through development which is facilitated rather than imposed and through integrated development approaches which take into account the teacher as person alongside the teacher as professional. Coaching is another example of professional development which is based on this thinking. It is becoming increasingly popular with teachers because it is perceived as being a less threatening approach to professional development.

Ultimately whatever type of development is used, if it values teachers then it is gifted and talented pupils who will benefit as their teachers become ever more effective resources for their pupils.

References

Clandinin, J. (1986) *Classroom Practice*. London: Falmer Press.

Clark, C. (1992) *Diary Writing and Analysis: an Emancipatory Tool for Teachers in Training*. Paper prepared for the British Educational Research Association Annual Conference, Stirling.

Clark, C. (1993) 'Changing teachers through telling stories', *Support for Learning* **8**(1), 31–4.

Easen, P. and Biott, C. (1994) *Collaborative Learning in Staffrooms and Classrooms*. London: David Fulton Publishers.

Freeman, J. (1998) *Educating the Very Able: Current International Research*. London: HMSO.

George, D. (1992) *The Challenge of the Able Child*. London: David Fulton Publishers.

Hanko, G. (1985) *Special Needs in Ordinary Classrooms*. Oxford: Blackwell.

Jordan, A. (1994) *Skills in Collaborative Classroom Consultation*. London: Routledge.

Knowles, J. G. (1992) 'Models for understanding pre-service and beginning teachers' biographies', in Goodson, I. F. (ed.) *Studying Teachers' Lives*. London: Routledge.

Louden, W. (1991) *Understanding Teaching*. London: Cassell.

McNiff, J. (1993) *Teaching as Learning: An Action Research Approach*. London: Routledge.

Reynolds, D. (1998) 'The school effectiveness mission has only just begun', *Times Educational Supplement*, 20 February.

CHAPTER 5

Strategies that encourage gifted and talented pupils and their teachers to become resources for learning

The *raison d'être* of this book is our belief that the effective use of resource facilitates and can improve learning. In this chapter we wish to widen the discussion about what constitutes resource and give in-depth consideration to ways, perhaps some of them new ways, in which resources can be used for maximum effect.

Resources for learning, of course, include more than books, new technologies and materials, important though these are. Without such resources, and increasingly without the Internet and its plethora of possibilities, teaching and learning would undoubtedly be impoverished and more difficult to execute efficiently. But we go to some length throughout this book to emphasise that *people resources* as much as *material resources* are equally valuable, available for use and ought to be used: in our view if they are not, the quality of education can be adversely affected.

All learners need resources and every pupil should be provided with appropriate resources. Gifted and talented pupils in particular make good use of resources. They are adept at exploiting resources for learning to the maximum because they are highly motivated and keen to get the most out of learning experiences. Many are so keen to investigate, problem solve and hypothesise that they have an insatiable need for resources to match the pace at which they learn.

Again, as for all pupils, the resource that is the mainstay of gifted and talented pupils is, of course, their teachers. Whatever resources are available to them, it is the teacher who:

- organises
- plans
- provides knowledge and skills
- guides
- engages with
- intervenes
- assesses
- works with – in other words mediates – the learning experiences.

The quality of the mediation depends on many factors, not least the competence of the teacher, but it is also greatly influenced by the relationship between the teacher and the learner. This is the cornerstone. If the teacher is going to be a resource for learning, the teacher-pupil relationship is crucial. At best it is somewhat different to the usual teacher-pupil relationship because there are specific attributes that enable a good relationship to develop.

> Gifted and talented pupils relate best to teachers who:
> know their subjects well
> treat them fairly
> have a sense of humour
> are enthusiastic
> teach creatively
> enjoy a challenge themselves
> and are confident socially as well as academically.

> Gifted and talented pupils:
> enjoy engaging with their teachers on a person-to-person level
> like to feel free to ask provocative questions
> question authority
> and have a particularly high level of comfort interacting with adults.
>
> (Clark and Shore 1998)

After carefully considering these attributes, for many teachers, the challenge of teaching gifted and talented pupils becomes more formidable. Nevertheless if teachers are to work successfully with gifted and talented pupils they need to be prepared to modify their usual teaching approach. Teachers who feel unable to work with gifted and talented pupils in the ways outlined above are doing a disservice to those pupils, the needs of whom, for too long, have been neglected.

But for those teachers who want to respond positively, a further benefit from achieving good relationships with gifted and talented pupils is that when they feel happy in class and their self-esteem is high, they are able to act as a resource not only for themselves but also for their peers and their teachers.

Then they feel comfortable about making a contribution to whole-class learning, to share ideas and thoughts with their peers and most probably they will contribute to raising the learning standards of all. Often social as well as academic benefits for the whole class will result. This is the kind of partnership that is surely a recipe for success in the classroom.

Twenty-five years ago Kerry (1978) noted that in mixed-ability settings in particular:

- teachers spent too much time with slow learners
- good pupils could get away with not working at an appropriate fast pace
- it was harder to cater for bright pupils in a mixed situation
- teachers were not doing their best for top pupils – work was aimed at the middle band

- the top third of pupils were not stretched
- bright pupils were more difficult to teach than other pupils.

How far might the same be said today? More recent reports (House of Commons 1999, DfEE 1999) suggest that even where learning is organised according to ability similar problems persist.

In such classrooms as Kerry describes it is very unlikely that either teachers or gifted and talented pupils can function effectively because suitable mediation of the learning environment is not possible.

The way to break out of this negative situation is to facilitate change in the classroom through flexibility. Flexibility is not easy to attain or maintain and some would argue that in the present educational context it is especially difficult. The underlying ethos in schools is authoritarian, based on a rigid National Curriculum and examination system, administered and taught by teachers who have been trained in a technical-competency mode which militates against creativity and spontaneity.

This environment does not obviously encourage innovative responses to teaching and learning which are prerequisites if gifted and talented pupils and their teachers are to succeed in breaking the barriers of underachievement and alienation. In this chapter we explore how to tackle this problem and in doing so unlock the potential which can flow from the people resources of both teacher and gifted and talented pupils. The key lies in flexible approaches to learning and the organisation of learning.

Teaching approaches, skills and techniques that are particularly appropriate for gifted and talented pupils

We have put forward the argument that gifted and talented pupils as well as teachers can become resources for teaching and learning if they are allowed to. It is up to teachers who are responsible for the learning that takes place in their classrooms to ensure that gifted and talented pupils are able to act as resources. This is more likely to happen if the learning experiences they undergo are suited to their needs. We are going to focus on ways to ensure that this happens.

Firstly teachers require a wider repertoire of teaching approaches and skills if they are to respond freshly and innovatively with spontaneity to gifted and talented pupils. Included in the chapters that follow are detailed descriptions of how to develop such teaching skills in information handling, problem solving and communication skills.

In this chapter generic teaching skills found to be popular with gifted and talented pupils are considered in some detail. Of course, not all of these will suit every teacher. That is not the purpose of the exercise. Nevertheless teachers should:

- be aware of the wide variety of teaching skills available to them;
- understand how to make use of them;

- experiment with those that appeal;
- if they 'work' for them, add them to the repertoire of skills they use regularly.

While most of us tend to repeat behaviours that we perceive as being successful in life in general, and it makes good sense to do so, in the more limited life in a classroom it can result in boredom for learners, especially gifted and talented learners. Variety is the spice of learning as well as life.

The Enrichment Triad Model

A tried and successfully tested approach to learning which appears to benefit gifted and talented pupils is Renzulli's Enrichment Triad Model (1977). Originally conceived in America it has been used worldwide because it is relatively easy to implement.

There are three levels of enrichment in this model.

Type 1

Type 1 has the goal of general enrichment and motivation. These also create an opportunity for teachers and pupils to discover high level interests and abilities which might not show up in day-to-day classroom life. Type 1 activities can be simple such as a recipe box of idea cards created by the teacher, and even by the pupils, of puzzles to think or write about; mathematical games or amusements; books or magazines with questions to ponder; or small research tasks that can be planned for the community within or outside the school. Type 1 activities are designed to capture children's interests and enhance motivation. They should be small projects, not requiring extended investments of time, anything from a few minutes to a few hours spread over several days. If a child chooses to extend the project, that is fine. Then, however, it becomes a Type 3.

Type 2

These provide pupils with the specific skills that they need to pursue independent learning individually or in small groups. Type 2 activities are normally taught in groups and might cover such skills as how to do a survey or conduct an interview; use photography or sound recording equipment; organise and summarise information; or critically read and evaluate newspaper reports. Computer and Internet skills can also be taught. Type 2 activities, under the supervision of the teacher, may be provided by parent volunteers, student teachers or mentors as well as by the teacher. They can be arranged on an *ad hoc* basis in response to pupil need, perhaps in order to enable them to move on to Type 3 activities.

Type 3

These are individual and small group independent projects on topics agreed and identified by the pupils with the teacher's agreement. When students have had some experience and success with Type 1 activities then it makes it easier for them to work on their own without disturbing the rest of the class. Typically these pupils may want to continue working on the projects outside of class time (Clark and Shore 1998).

Opportunity should be given to share this Enrichment Triad work with the class, other pupils, parents and school visitors. Renzulli also argues that this work should be undertaken for the pleasure of learning and while it is fair to report accurately on what and how well the pupils learned, he considers marks and grades less important.

However, in the current educational setting here, unless this work is done in after-school clubs, Saturday morning classes or summer schools, it probably will be necessary to assess the work because it took place during school time and most probably will be an extension or enrichment of the National Curriculum. Although the activities of whatever type would have to be linked in some way with the National Curriculum it is worth pointing out that the process of devising such activities in itself can be a release for teachers. It requires them to think beyond the routine, the ordinary and encourage them to be more creative in their ideas. It also provides the pupils with the means to be proactive in their learning because they can be encouraged:

- to think of ways to research;
- to problem solve;
- to ask questions about the topic of particular interest to them;
- to want to acquire certain skills to enable them to cope with data or produce evidence.

We know from our own experience that the ideas the pupils come up with are usually good, sometimes outstanding and occasionally inspirational. By giving the pupils their heads, allowing them to use their imagination and ability, we have found that they have helped us to be creative and innovative in our teaching. In other words they were a resource to us.

The Enrichment Triad Model is an excellent example of how to adapt the curriculum so that both teachers and their gifted and talented pupils can become resources for each other. It is also straightforward enough for any teachers who are starting out on this road to try.

The Cognitive Apprenticeship Model

This model is based within a *social context for learning* which seeks to motivate and encourage a positive orientation to learning through:

- **situated learning** so that pupils see the purpose of the learning and how it can be applied;
- **community of practice** which provides the chance to talk with others about different ways to accomplish the tasks and is facilitated by sharing projects and experiences;

- **intrinsic motivation** often strengthened by pupils setting their own goals;
- **cooperation** encouraged by working with others in pairs or groups, sometimes in competition depending on the circumstance.

(Higgins in Eyre and McClure 2001)

The model also suggests the following ways to develop *expert performance*:

- **coaching**: where the teacher observes pupils carrying out tasks and offers feedback and prompts to bring their performance closer to that of an expert;
- **scaffolding**: where the teacher provides support for pupils while requiring them to take steps on the learning ladder by themselves, knowing that if they fall they will be caught. In other words, the teacher provides the stimulus for learning, gets the pupils involved in learning, intervenes to move the learners on if necessary, encourages the learners to take risks – to step outside what they are familiar with – but is there to support them as required. Over time the amount of support can be appropriately reduced until pupils are confident to work on their own;
- **articulation**: where the pupils are given the opportunity to explain their reasoning and make explicit their knowledge;
- **reflection:** where the pupils are given an opportunity to compare their learning and thinking processes with others including the teacher;
- **exploration**: where the pupils have to come up with their own problem-solving solutions so that they become better questioners and investigators.

This model, like Renzulli's model, can be used across the curriculum. Its attractiveness for use with gifted and talented pupils arises out of the shared involvement of both teacher and pupil in a more equal learning partnership than is common in many classrooms. But also it emphasises the importance of acquiring skills to a high level deemed by the pupil as well as the teacher to be useful. Collaboration is stressed as is the importance of investigation and problem solving. Sharing knowledge is valued in both models but it is the Cognitive Apprenticeship Model that provides the opportunity quite explicitly for pupils to talk about, not only what they learned, but how they think they learned it. By doing so it may well help them to learn better. This is a key aspect to which not much attention is given in busy classrooms.

Gifted and talented pupils may be good learners but it is more than likely that they could become better learners if they understood more about how they learn. Through articulation and reflection as described in this model they could begin to do that, which is one of the reasons why this model is becoming of increasing interest to teachers of gifted and talented pupils.

While curriculum adaptation models such as these are excellent vehicles for promoting variety in teaching and learning as well as developing both teacher and pupil understanding of how learning occurs and how learning can be enhanced, they may well be too all-encompassing for some colleagues. Undoubtedly they would be helpful in reaching our goal of using the teacher and gifted and talented pupils as resources for learning but you can only go as fast as you are able along the road. What follows therefore is some suggestions which complement much of what is contained in these models but which are less comprehensive.

Other ways forward with gifted and talented pupils

Kerry and Kerry (1997), for instance, list these guidelines for teaching gifted and talented pupils:

- new knowledge should not be presented in isolation but linked with prior learning and within a conceptual framework;
- *problem posing* as well as *problem solving* should be used to stimulate thinking;
- appropriate technical language should be used as necessary – do not simplify;
- pupils should be encouraged to compare old and new learning and ideas with their peers;
- pupils should be provided with own time rewards so that they can work on their own projects, agreed by the teacher.

All, or indeed any, of these would help teachers to provide a varied and more appropriate diet for gifted and talented pupils. Other possibilities include the strategy of *demonstrating the expert thinking of gifted and talented pupils* (Clark and Shore 1998). These are useful in a number of ways, not least because they provide the teacher with some understanding of how pupils are thinking as well as what it is teachers need to model to the pupils in order to improve their thinking. They also can help pupils to understand how they think and thus enhance their problem-solving skills.

Here are some examples:

> a) *Pupils can be asked to report back at the end of a lesson about the main ideas learnt from the lesson. They can then try to interconnect these ideas and be asked to explain the connections. This concept map improves their ability to solve problems where all the elements are not set out; they have to think through all the steps.*
>
> b) *Pupils can be asked to talk about what they are thinking as they solve a problem. This can be done on a board in front of the rest of the class, or with pupils working in pairs, or in an individual interview with the pupil. What this does is to enable people to slow down their thinking process so that when problem solving they can begin to formulate a plan rather than simply follow a trial and error process. It can also encourage them to be more flexible in their approach so that when faced with a difficult task, they may be prepared to pursue different roads. Using the*

> *knowledge from this exercise the teacher can model thinking processes which would help them to improve their thinking. Eventually if a class becomes practised at this approach pupils can do this for each other*

Holderness (in Eyre and McClure 2001: 45) provides *an enquiry-based model for learning* which is useful in any subject and merits consideration. Devised by the International Schools Curriculum Project (1999) it is designed to be culturally open-ended so that it can be used in any context. The framework focuses on the following questions:

- What is it like?
- How does it work?
- Why is it like it is?
- How is it changing?
- How is it connected to other things?
- What are the points of view?
- How do we know?

Questions like these are stimulating for gifted and talented pupils and encourage them to use different types of thinking. They are a useful extension to the repertoire of the teacher of gifted and talented pupils.

Other possibilities include the introduction of *the notion of cognitive conflict* into the learning situation. This is when the learner is faced with information or a situation that directly challenges their understanding. They are confronted with the fact that what they believe to be so is not so and they are forced to adapt their thinking. Particularly well known is the work of Shayer and Adey (1981) in science in secondary schools.

Another idea is *pupil-led projects* within and without National Curriculum Guidelines. This is a good example of pupils acting as a resource. We introduce this approach by:

> using concept maps to find out what pupils already know about the topic we propose to teach.
>
> Having discussed the concept maps with the pupils to ascertain in greater depth what they know rather than what they might think they know, we use the same maps to elicit what the pupils would like to know more about.
> Guidelines for the project are then agreed regarding aims, objectives, amount of time to be spent.
>
> The pupils work independently as individuals, or if appropriate in pairs or in groups, in class or out of the classroom in the school learning centre, ICT facility or library, whichever is available.

Regular meetings are held:

- to check out progress;
- to praise for effort and/or outcome;
- to pick up on issues that need to be highlighted;
- to clarify, or to be precise to make comments, or put forward ideas which help the pupils to clarify for themselves any questions or issues;
- to ask challenging questions which will encourage them to go further;
- to evaluate the learning outcomes and the learning experience.

On completion of the project, the pupils present their findings to the rest of the class interconnecting it with the class project.

This technique requires highly skilled intervention by the teacher so that the learning is managed in a way that encourages partnership between teacher and pupil. While it is not appropriate for the teacher to be overly dominant in this pupil-led activity, it is necessary for the teacher to manage the learning activity and act as mediator of the learning by asking questions like:

'Now that is interesting, why did you say that?'
'Can you explain again your thinking about . . .'
'If you do that, then won't it be likely that this will happen?'
'Is there a completely different way of looking at that? What if you say . . .?'
'Can you justify that view?'
'Does this remind you of anything else we've looked at?'

Questions similar to these, which assume the teacher as much as the pupil is in learning mode, are helpful. But there is no reason at all why the teacher should not provide information or knowledge as and when required or suggest to the pupils where they might find out what they want to know. They will certainly look to the teacher for this kind of expert input possibly framed in conversations that are more like adult-to-adult transactions than adult-to-child.

Pupils at the government-organised summer schools commented that they enjoyed working with teachers who did not act like teachers. This is interesting because many of the summer school tutors were not school teachers as such, they were advisory teachers, college lecturers and specialists. Was their approach to learning and were their relationships with the pupils more like the pupil-led, democratic learning interactions described above?

Other ideas which may be helpful

If gifted pupils have no problems with homework, allow them to continue and make progress with their work at their own speed and spend time with those pupils who have problems. There is nothing worse for gifted pupils than to have to sit in class hearing an explanation for the third or fourth time which they grasped first time around.

....

Advise that if they have worked through several straightforward examples correctly they should go on to the more complex examples rather than spending valuable time practising the same kind of thing over and over again. Gifted and talented learners do need to practise in order to learn but they require less practice than their peers.

....

Think about *answering time*. Gifted and talented pupils benefit from being given time to think about an answer before responding. Too often a quick response is a superficial response. Give the class a couple of minutes to think about their answers; they could even jot down notes before replying. This is not a technique to be used all the time, as it might impede the flow of a lesson, but for certain questions which demand more thought it is worth trying. From our experience the quality of the answers tends to improve. Also it is often effective to ask the pupil who responds a second question. This appears to encourage more in-depth and thoughtful replies.

....

Some further ideas

Collaborate with LEA gifted and talented specialist teachers or the specialist within your own school or cluster. Collaborative teaching ventures are usually enjoyable and useful. This could become part of your professional development programme for the academic year.

....

Providing gifted and talented pupils with more time to work in greater depth and/ or breadth is an aspect of flexible working that is well worth considering. For instance, school work could be linked with after-school work in clubs, Masterclasses or summer schools.

....

Learning beyond the classroom is another way to introduce variety and flexibility into the learning situation:

- Make use of the school study centre, or cluster ICT centre.
- Use online facilities such as the Cambridge University Xcalibre programme.

- Visit and work in the local specialist colleges with older students for art, dance, sport or music.
- Bring specialists into the school such as actors, dancers, potters, lawyers, politicians . . . the list is endless.

....

Add to the variety of subjects on offer, possibly taking up suggestions from the pupils. This could be a way to involve the alienated gifted underachiever bored with regular curriculum offerings. Subjects such as Latin, Greek, archaeology, psychology, astronomy seem to be popular choices.

....

The following suggestions may also help teachers to further their knowledge for teaching gifted and talented pupils.

Work in partnership with independent schools which are specifically geared to working with gifted and talented pupils.
Shadow their teachers.
Collaborate on projects that are mutually advantageous to pupils from both schools.

On a regular basis attend lectures and seminars on leading edge developments in your specialist subjects so that you are up to date and feel confident that you are in touch with the latest thinking.

Use the National Curriculum Guidelines for subject extension possibilities and the extended questions in public examinations to provide ideas of how to extend and enrich the curriculum.

All of these ideas facilitate flexible approaches to teaching and learning, approaches that help gifted and talented pupils to remain enthusiastic about learning. We need to be mindful that some become turned off by school life. They can become frustrated, difficult to handle, unmotivated and play truant like any other group of learners who feel alienated from the system. The strategies discussed in this chapter could go some way to prevent this from happening. Variety and flexibility of approach make classrooms into greatly enriched learning environments. Such flexibility maximises the use of teachers and pupils as resources. In the next chapter more will be said about how teachers and schools can plan to make this happen.

The remainder of this chapter will, however, focus on observation in the classroom – a bedrock for change and development. In our view this technique is the fulcrum of the processes which inform teacher thinking and action in the classroom.

Observation

Why observe?

The main reason for undertaking observation in the classroom is to get to know the pupil better. What this means is that taken together with examination, test and project results over time the teacher will gain more accurate insight into the levels of functioning and rate of progress of pupils than would otherwise be likely.

As well as information about academic outcomes observation can provide data on the equally important social, emotional and physical aspects of development and learning, all of which interact and affect each other.

Also observation can give the teacher clues about the manner in which the pupil learns and the way she/he prefers to learn. Teachers can then discuss these matters with pupils with the aim of exploiting their strengths and improving their weaknesses. More of this later.

Observation can also highlight learning difficulties. The obvious learning difficulties such as spelling, handwriting, grammar or reading should have been picked up by the continuous assessment and monitoring procedures used throughout school life. But more subtle problems such as:

- how pupils organise their learning;
- the use of different strategies in reading to suit specific tasks;
- how to modify an essentially aural learning task into a visual learning task if that is the preferred way of working;

are not so easily picked up except through systematic observation. But they are important if standards of learning are to improve. Following observation, teachers can feed back to the pupil and, if necessary, coach the pupil, possibly through modelling, so that ways of learning can be improved.

This might include the teaching of study skills which can be taught and applied within a meaningful context or higher order thinking skills.

It is often wrongly assumed that very bright pupils are highly competent learners. They may be, but they may not. All learners can improve their learning skills to a greater or lesser extent and for most learners there is a difference when they are taught how to learn effectively. The development of metacognition, which is what this is, offers a great challenge to gifted and talented pupils. It can help them to help themselves, in other words to become independent learners.

Among the information that we have ascertained about gifted and talented pupils through observation over the years is the following:

- some prefer to work alone;
- others want to work with another high-flier;
- some like to work in a group where each has a unique task agreed by all;
- others prefer a mix of all of these depending on the activity.

In each of these settings they tend to complete the task successfully when they work in the preferred way. This is not to say that they are always allowed to work in the same way. The teacher may have other reasons for organising learning differently, for instance if social integration is a primary aim then mixed-ability groupings are preferable. Or it may be important to do whole-class teaching to introduce or conclude a project. However, teachers who make use of observation data to inform their planning generally ensure that the preferred way of working for gifted and talented pupils is made available to them on a regular basis.

Observation of the pupil working in these different settings can also elicit why the pupil prefers to work in that setting – is it for academic or social reasons or both?

Information about how he/she learns best, whether through processes that are oral, visual, aural, kinaesthetic or a combination of these, can also be ascertained.

Other possible questions which observation can cast light on include:

- Does this pupil have an 'ideal' length of time for learning?
- What kind of task does the pupil prefer – a task where he/she is given:
  - a starting point
  - an ending point
  - an intermediate point?

There is no suggestion that the pupil would always work on one type of task but again the teacher could ensure that from time to time he/she could learn through the type of task that stimulates him/her most.

Does the pupil enjoy sharing work outcomes with others? By choice how would he/she do this? Make a display, give a presentation, make a video, write a computer program?

An analysis of work outcomes and observation data such as that described above means that the teacher has vital detail about gifted and talented pupils which will help them to tailor-make appropriate provision for them in the classroom. With this information the teacher can make use of the ideas put forward, for example, in Eyre (1997) among others:

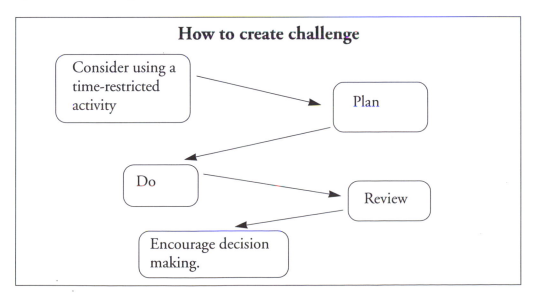

Making time for observation

Teachers who have read this chapter with interest thus far will no doubt be keen to know how, among everything else that busy teachers have to do, is it possible to find the time to observe.

It is certainly easiest in classrooms where:

- the pupils are already used to working independently for periods of time, either as individuals, in pairs or in groups;

or in classrooms where:

- there is regular additional planned help from other colleagues, either teachers or classroom assistants; or trainee teachers, nursery nurses or parents;
- during special projects where, for instance, outside specialists such as the cluster lead gifted and talented coordinator, or the school coordinator can teach alongside the class or subject teacher;
- classroom-based research is part of the professional development programme for the individual teacher; the school in which this takes place might agree to provide support which enables the teacher to undertake observation for research data;
- teachers can obtain research bursaries from the DfES to do classroom-based research, perhaps some of this money being used to fund a teacher partner.

Such research can be extremely valuable. An example of a teacher research project which can provide useful information is the following (Clark and Callow 1998):

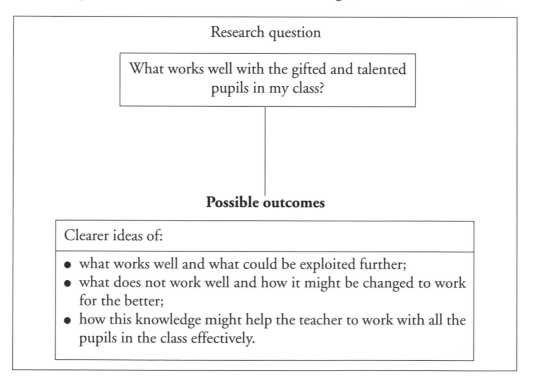

Research question

What works well with the gifted and talented pupils in my class?

Possible outcomes

Clearer ideas of:

- what works well and what could be exploited further;
- what does not work well and how it might be changed to work for the better;
- how this knowledge might help the teacher to work with all the pupils in the class effectively.

To make observation happen it needs to be seen as essential by teachers otherwise the effort required to organise it will not be made. From our experience and that of many students who have used observation, it is worth it. Observation is a teacher-friendly technique of potentially great practical as well as theoretical use. Each day all teachers make use of informal, if not formal, observation to build up a picture of pupils but mostly they do not make the best use of the information received. Few teachers write up their observations systematically or analyse them.

Thus many useful observations are lost because it is impossible for teachers to recall the myriad interactions between themselves and their pupils and between pupil and pupil. It is not, of course, essential to remember every tiny detail of what a pupil does throughout a busy day; that is not what observation aims to do. Rather the observation is usually focused on particular tasks which the teacher considers to be of special interest.

These tasks have to be designed so that the observer can see things happening; therefore an activity that is entirely mental would be less rewarding than one that involved 'doing something' which could be observed.

Also the observation does not necessarily have to be done throughout an entire lesson; a shorter period of time might well be satisfactory. It depends on the reasons for doing the observation which need to be carefully thought through beforehand.

Within this context teachers have reported to us that observation:

- has helped them to evaluate a lesson;
- has enabled them to plan forward;
- has provided useful information about particular pupils to ensure that their learning needs are being satisfactorily met.

In addition the observation has been especially helpful in pointing up those gifted and talented pupils who appeared to be doing very well but in actual fact were 'coasting'.

It has also highlighted aspects of the task that have delighted and stimulated the pupil more than might have been expected. Teachers have then been able to exploit this more fully.

Some teachers have shared the observation data with the gifted and talented pupils themselves in order to plan where to go next.

This seems to work best when:

- the pupils' opinions are sought about the interpretation of the data and ways forward;
- the decisions they make are real and make a difference to what happens to them day by day in the classroom;
- they can relate to the teacher whom they respect in a person-to-person way rather than a child-to-adult way;
- they can engage in discussion about concepts such as learning and theories of learning arising from the data.

This removes a lot of guesswork out of the equation. It enables teachers to present satisfying learning experiences to pupils. The observations and pupil interviews do, of course, take time, but even on a termly basis they can improve the quality of learning. Pupils should feel more satisfied because their work will be appropriately planned to meet their individual needs. They ought to be in a positive frame of mind and produce evidence of successful learning.

Observation is not a magic wand but it is a useful resource which is greatly underused. Teachers who work in formal classrooms where learning is strongly teacher-led will find it challenging and perhaps less satisfactory to make use of the technique especially as we envisage it being used. But clearly from our work (Clark and Callow 1998) it helps teachers to begin to understand the complexities of classroom life. It can also lead teachers to question their own perceptions about themselves as people, themselves as teachers and their pupils.

Using the evidence they have collected teachers begin to understand themselves and their pupils better. Ultimately such information ought to lead to more effective teaching. Nevertheless observation, as any other technique, will not always be feasible or desirable for all teachers.

How to observe

There are many ways to do classroom observation. Some are very different from others. Perhaps the greatest divergence is between structured and unstructured approaches.

Highly structured approaches are used to focus on the frequency, duration and intensity of certain behaviours to the exclusion of all else, whereas unstructured observations try to paint a broader picture in order to include as many cues and clues as possible which, hopefully, will make it easier to understand what is going on. One type is not better than the other. What is important is that there is an appropriate match between the type and the aims of the observation.

Overall we favour the unstructured approach to classroom observation because it is teacher-friendly and inclusive by which we mean that, if it is done properly, the data will include cues or clues that otherwise might be missed and that have proved to be extremely useful.

How to proceed with unstructured observation

First of all decide:

What do I want to observe?
Why?
When am I going to do it?
What special arrangements if any do I have to make (it may be necessary to involve other personnel)?
If this is an unusual occurrence how do I explain it to the pupils?

Does the Head know?
Is it necessary to inform parents?
Am I clear about how to do an unstructured observation?
Have I chosen an appropriate task?
Have I planned the lesson so that it is satisfactory for all pupils not only those whom I am observing?

We have found that using observation on a regular basis makes life easier for all concerned. One thing that makes the whole process more straightforward is taking the sense of novelty out of the situation. If it becomes part and parcel of what goes on in the classroom on a regular basis then everyone begins to feel more comfortable.

Most definitely we have not restricted classroom observation solely to gifted and talented pupils. Teachers can benefit from observing all pupils because it elicits useful information about their learning which can improve how they learn.

Pupils are usually not overly concerned once they know what you are doing and why you are doing it. If you explain that you are watching to see how they tackle the task or how they work together in order to help them do better work, this usually seems to satisfy them.

Careful consideration needs to be given to where you position yourself while observing: sitting too close to those being observed, you become threatening and are likely to be asked questions by the pupils about the task. But too far away and you will not be able to hear and see what is going on.

Unless you are fortunate enough to have another teacher colleague in the class with you who is prepared to take responsibility for overseeing the class while you undertake the observation, then as the teacher in charge it will remain your responsibility to see that all is well in the classroom. This needs to be taken into account with regard to positioning.

Both the pupils and their parents or guardians will find feedback about the observations helpful and it is probably a natural expectation that if you have been observed the observer will talk to you about what he/she has found. If at the regular parent/teacher meetings you can feed back data to parents which they can exploit in order to help their child then this too becomes part of the process of educating gifted and talented pupils successfully.

The pupil interviews which follow the observations should be couched in positive terms but should also include appropriate challenges for the learner or if necessary coaching in new approaches to learning which he/she might employ to develop effective study and/or thinking skills.

It almost goes without saying that as with any skill used by teachers in the classroom, observation must be well done. Like any other skill, practice will improve the teacher's ability to undertake unstructured observation. There are many different types of observation. We tend to make use of unstructured observation because it provides a broader picture of what is happening. In unstructured observation the aim is to write down in script form precisely what was said and done without extraneous comment. Thus:

John (with a frown): I'm really stuck. If that is 6 and this is 7 then what does that tell us about this number? It's unconnected, it seems to me.
Alison: There's got to be a connection. Let's see. Now just listen, give me a minute.

is appropriate.

But the following would not be permitted:

Observer: I think she is getting annoyed with him. She'd rather have the time on her own to solve this problem. He's too impatient and impulsive.

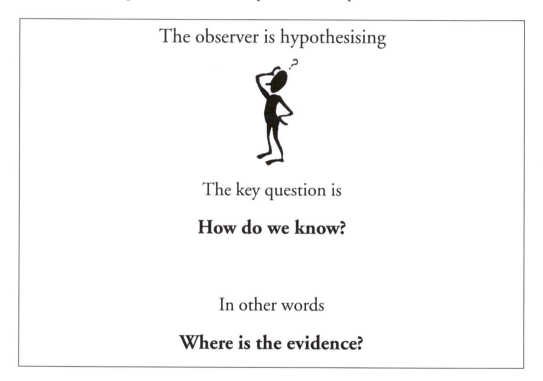

The observer is hypothesising

The key question is

How do we know?

In other words

Where is the evidence?

Now if this happened:

Alison removed the work card from John, turned her back on him and said, 'Just give me a few minutes of peace and quiet,' that would be a different matter. The observer has evidence.

Most people write the data by hand or increasingly the use of a laptop, where one is available, is becoming commonplace. Over time some observers use symbols or parts of words as a kind of shorthand instead.

The next issue for discussion is how the observer decides what to write down. It will prove impossible to write everything down and it is not possible to ask for an action replay. Firstly all observers make choices about what they record, based partly on what they remember and what they find of special interest. This is not necessarily a problem. Try to write down as much as you can. A script is useful which is why some observers have tried to tape-record observations but this has technical as well as other problems. Some pupils cannot get used to having a microphone on the table. Also important non-verbal cues are lost unless the observer is at the same time noting things down.

The best advice is to focus on things that are most obviously connected with the aims of the observation. Remember it is only possible to do the best one can and whatever you manage to collect is rather more than would normally be available if you were not doing the observation.

If when you analyse the data you feel you need to corroborate certain aspects because you were unable to write down everything that was said and done, plan to do another observation of a similar activity and compare and contrast the behaviours and outcomes. This might help.

It is advisable to rewrite your observation notes as soon after the event as possible while it is fresh in your mind. The next stage is to make copies for the two colleagues who have previously agreed to be involved. In fact we have found this works well when you can do this for each other in a reciprocal cycle such as was described in Chapter 4 on professional development. All three of you should go through the script without prior discussion, underlining whatever strikes you as being of interest. This might be something unusual, unexpected, perplexing or amusing. It might be something that is repeated or not included when you thought it would be. It could be anything.

As soon as it is feasible the three of you should meet for an agreed amount of time. We usually find half an hour acceptable. The person who did the observation leads the discussion going through the script systematically.

What you will be looking for in the first instance are points that stood out to all three of you and that you all three interpreted in the same way. Where this happens you can be fairly sure that your perception of what happened and why is reasonably accurate. This is an example of *triangulation,* a technique in research methodology which suggests that the results, in this case the interpretations, are rigorous.

Equally, points picked out but interpreted differently by each of the analysts give rise to discussions that provide alternative viewpoints which may be of great use to the teacher-observer.

Where the analysts picked out completely different points, this too can open up discussion about what the important issues and interactions were.

In many ways the really important thing is to talk about teaching and learning and try to find out as much about it as it happens.

Unstructured observation attempts to systematise the collection and analysis of data about teaching and learning and meaningfully contextualise what could otherwise be construed as theoretical and less relevant to the practice-orientated teacher.

Providing emotional support

This chapter has outlined ways in which teachers can act as a major resource to their pupils as well as ways in which gifted and talented pupils can act as a resource for themselves and their peers. If this is to happen a wide range of teaching approaches alongside flexible responses to the organisation and management of learning is necessary. Observation is an underlying skill which guides the teacher towards making tailor-made responses appropriate for individual gifted and talented pupils. It is therefore an essential skill in the teacher's repertoire. In order to facilitate the education of gifted and talented pupils to the highest level they have to be challenged – highly involved, heavily committed and greatly enjoy their educational experiences – these skills and strategies go some way to make this happen.

Perhaps we should end on a note of caution. There can be a downside to gifted and talented pupils acting as resources. They can be exploited. They can find themselves being leading lights all the time. They can be used as coaches for other pupils too often. For example, they can be responsible for raising standards in class by constantly being asked to give class presentations to extend the learning of their peers. This means they are put under great pressure to perform. They can be expected to compete all the time and in everything they do. They can be expected to participate in every aspect of school life and excel in all. Remember they may not always want to be star turns. They may not want to be older than their years every minute of every day. They may not want to be pressurised by peers, teachers and parents.

This issue requires careful consideration. Gifted and talented pupils require emotional support just as other pupils. In some schools this is provided by mentors, that is teachers chosen by the pupils themselves, teachers with whom they are comfortable to discuss how they feel about school in general and any specific issues. Some schools timetable regular appointments between mentors and pupils.

The school that neglects the all-round well-being of gifted and talented pupils will have far less resources to utilise and the end result is that gifted and talented pupils are less likely to achieve what they are capable of achieving.

References

Clark, C. and Callow, R. (1998) *Educating Able Children*. London: David Fulton Publishers.

Clark, C. and Shore, B. (1998) *Educating Students with High Ability*. Paris: UNESCO.

Department for Education and Employment (DfEE) (1999) *Excellence in Cities*. London: HMSO.

Eyre, D. (1997) *Able Children in Ordinary Schools*. London: David Fulton Publishers.

Higgins, C. (2001) 'Information and Communication Technology', in Eyre, D. and McClure, L. (2001) *Curriculum Provision for the Gifted and Talented in the Primary School.* London: David Fulton Publishers, 117–40.

Holderness, J. (2001) 'English' in Eyre, D. and McClure, L. (2001) *Curriculum Provision for the Gifted and Talented in the Primary School.* London: David Fulton Publishers 28–64.

House of Commons Education and Employment Committee (1999), Third Report, 'Highly Able Children'. London: HMSO.

Kerry, T. (1978) 'Bright pupils in mixed ability classes', *British Educational Research Journal* 4(20), 103–11.

Kerry, T. and Kerry, C. (1997) 'Teaching the more able; primary and secondary education practice compared', *Education Today* 47, 11–16.

Kerry, T. and Kerry, C. (2000) 'The centrality of teaching skills in improving able pupil education', *Educating Able Children* 4(20), 13–19.

Renzulli, J. S. (1977) *Enrichment Triad Model: A guide for developing defensible programs for the gifted and talented.* Mansfield Center, Connecticut, USA: Creative Learning Press.

Shayer, M. and Adey, P. (1981) *Towards a Science of Science Teaching.* Oxford: Heinemann.

CHAPTER 6

Planning for gifted and talented pupils by teachers and schools

Planning at school level

In the last chapter we stressed the point that flexibility and variety in teacher response together with the effective use of resources are essential if appropriate provision is to be made for gifted and talented pupils. However, these issues are not the responsibility of teachers alone; they also require thought and action by schools as a whole. The implications for schools are far reaching: as an example let us take the support teachers require in order to do observation which we described as providing a bedrock for successful work in the classroom with gifted and talented pupils. Teachers need time to:

- plan the observation
- undertake the observation
- write up the data
- analyse the data with two colleagues
- decide on ways forward.

Other colleagues might also be involved in working with the class while the teacher observes. Clearly all this has a financial, time and resource cost.

If the observations are to be part of the teacher's professional development programme then this has to be discussed and agreed with the school's Coordinator for Professional Development – a further time commitment. Then, in order to be both effective and give value for money, the Coordinator should attempt to incorporate this individual's project within the overall school plan for professional development relating to gifted and talented pupils. In this way far more colleagues can benefit from the initiative. And so it goes on.

If such initiatives are to happen they are dependent on decisions made at school level, agreed throughout senior management and ideally supported by all staff. Initiatives are far more successful if they have the overwhelming support of the staff and those for gifted and talented pupils are no exception.

In some gifted and talented pupil initiatives acceleration has been used.

In others, time has been allocated for Renzulli Type 3 projects within, as well as without, school time.

In yet others, pupils are moved into ability settings – all in the interest of increasing the flexibility of response of teachers to gifted and talented pupils.

Each of these and many of the other ideas suggested to improve the education of gifted and talented pupils require in-depth discussion at senior management level because there are major implications, not only with regard to the organisation of learning but for resource allocation, the school ethos and professional development among other things. Even if senior staff are convinced of the efficacy of an idea, staff too need to be involved and committed to the changes because a number, if not many of them, are probably going to be affected by the decision on a daily basis.

Even five years ago many schools would not have thought it necessary to discuss the education of gifted and talented pupils. They believed they did not have any gifted pupils. Times have changed and increasingly following the lead of EiC schools, in line with government thinking, just as all schools have pupils with special educational needs so too do all schools have gifted and talented pupils. These are the two ends of the education spectrum. The term 'gifted' is now used as a relative term in this country and not given only to those who score a specific high percentage in an intelligence quotient (IQ) test. There is increasing interest in identifying and supporting pupils who have potential but are unmotivated or handicapped because they have a special educational problem. In EiC schools 5% to 10% of each year group has to be identified as gifted and talented.

Two thirds of that cohort comprises pupils with academic ability in one or more subjects of the statutory curriculum other than art, music and PE, while one third comprises pupils with ability in art, PE, sport, music, drama or creative art.

The provision made for gifted and talented pupils is included in the inspection mandate of Ofsted and schools are expected to have a school policy and a Key Person or Gifted and Talented Coordinator.

Thus schools cannot easily avoid taking seriously their responsibility for gifted and talented pupils. Nor can they take the view that these pupils will get on anyway without additional attention and support; they have to acknowledge their right to an appropriate education. Although many schools will be able to benefit in the short to medium term from government-funded initiatives such as those described in Chapter 2, they also need to differentiate their own regular resources with care to ensure that each pupil obtains what is necessary to function successfully. Roaf and Bines (1989) state that schools need to target resources at individuals rather than classes or even groups, otherwise valuable resources are wasted.

We think the same attitude should prevail with teacher development, so that whenever it is feasible individuals and small groups should be targeted rather than religiously using a blanket approach to cover all staff.

Schools that differentiate their use of resources in this way are good examples of inclusive schools which seek to support all pupils and teachers appropriately to enable them to achieve their maximum. Characteristics of these schools, described by Her Majesty's Inspectorate ten years ago (HMI 1992), endure today; they include:

- a high level of commitment at senior management level to the education of gifted and talented pupils;
- the involvement of the majority of members of staff in planning programmes for gifted and talented pupils as well as in appropriate professional development;
- the appointment and active involvement of a Gifted and Talented Coordinator;
- a willingness to focus on the individual through the differentiation of tasks;
- the careful monitoring of individual progress;
- teachers with a deep understanding of their subjects;
- teachers with high expectations of learners;
- an appropriate choice of resources including ICT;
- the encouragement of learners to take responsibility for their own learning;
- variation in pace, teaching style and classroom organisation;
- a stimulating learning environment;
- a good local education authority.

The Gifted and Talented Coordinator

A review in February 2002 by the DfES commented that in the schools that are most successful with gifted and talented pupils the Gifted and Talented Coordinator is either a member of the Senior Management Team or has a senior management 'sponsor' to facilitate direct contact with the Coordinator.

Kathy August, Education Adviser at the DfES for the Standards and Effectiveness Unit, wrote in the October 2001 issue of the DfES Newsletter that:

☞ **the essential ingredients for success in EiC schools are enthusiasm and committed coordination at all levels of schools, cluster and partnership.**

She also noted that Coordinators need:

- time to do the job;
- support to influence;
- access to key people within the school including Heads of Department, the timetabler and the Assessment Coordinator.

Furthermore we suggest that Coordinators be given the chance to undergo professional development of the type described in Chapters 3 and 4 which will give them an opportunity to begin to explore and understand their own beliefs, values and assumptions about gifted and talented pupils.

They then will be in a much stronger position to offer the same kind of experience to their colleagues. It is essential to do this if hearts and minds are to be won over. Not all colleagues are likely to agree about the way forward but at least time will have been spent coming to terms with where they stand on the issue of the education of gifted and talented pupils. As well as this, Integrated Professional Development will provide Coordinators with leading edge knowledge of how to teach gifted and talented pupils holistically so that their emotional as well as academic needs are taken into account. This too can be shared with colleagues who, when the issue of gifted and talented pupils is first raised, often ask questions such as:

'How do I identify gifted and talented pupils?'
'Once identified, how do I teach them?'
'How will I manage the rest of the class and at the same time spend time and effort on the gifted and talented group?'
'Do they require anything different to other pupils particularly with regard to emotional support?'

In Chapter 7 there is a lot of information about starting up provision for gifted and talented pupils which answers these questions.

In schools that have adopted the inclusive approach, the Coordinator for Gifted and Talented Pupils works with the whole staff to write the school's policy on gifted and talented education. As soon as this is done in some schools many, if not all, the teachers start to plan the provision for gifted and talented pupils which is to be developed over the medium term. This ensures that the policy is actioned almost immediately: thus it is put into practice and not left on the shelf and both the policy and provision are reviewed on an annual basis. The policy formulation exercise and the planning of provision are an integral part of the professional development programme for the gifted and talented cohort. Following these activities the Coordinator has responsibility for monitoring and reviewing what happens during the year, taking into account the comments and experiences of staff as well as pupils.

It is imperative that schools choose a teacher of the highest calibre as the Coordinator for Gifted and Talented Pupils, especially those schools that aim to be inclusive and function in the way described above. That person has to have the ability to engage with issues and ideas as well as colleagues, parents and pupils at many different levels and ways. Their skills should include the abilities:

- to take the lead in the formulation and periodic review of the school policy for gifted and talented pupils;
- to take the lead in setting up, evaluating and monitoring school-wide provision for gifted and talented pupils;
- to plan and lead sophisticated professional development experiences;
- to set up, maintain and develop liaison with parents of gifted and talented pupils;

- to set up, maintain and develop strong links with the governors concerning matters appertaining to gifted and talented pupils;
- to liaise with cluster colleagues and outside agencies about gifted and talented pupil initiatives.

In order to be able to do these things well the school should make sure that the Coordinator:

- has ongoing additional and appropriate professional development experiences;
- has sufficient prime time to liaise with colleagues, parents and outside agencies;
- ideally he/she should be a member of the Senior Management Team in order to influence planning decisions made about gifted and talented pupils.

☞ **In addition the Gifted and Talented Coordinator needs to have experience in teaching gifted and talented pupils and be given the resources to develop provision within and without school.**

The Coordinator needs to be:

- a role model for other staff
- enthusiastic
- confident
- in a position to gain additional qualification in gifted and talented education
- able to relate positively to colleagues, governors, parents and pupils.

Schools together with teachers therefore share a great deal of the burden of responsibility for the education of gifted and talented pupils. If gifted and talented pupils are not seen to be a priority by the head teacher and Senior Management Team then the majority of teachers in the school will not make them so.

Resource allocation too makes all the difference in the world as to what teachers can do; if resources are not readily available then initiatives will often flounder. If there is no clear policy and plan for provision for gifted and talented pupils then things will tend to drift. Most particularly if there is no Coordinator for Gifted and Talented Pupils then impetus will not be sustained.

A strand in every school development plan therefore needs to be dedicated to gifted and talented education. Financial, management and organisational planning decisions in the long term as well as the medium term and short term need to be made if the education of gifted and talented pupils is to progress. In other words strategic planning at the highest level led by a committed head teacher makes all the difference as to how well a school is able to serve its gifted and talented pupils.

The most enlightened form of school planning in our view is that which incorporates the opinions of teachers, governors, parents and pupils as far as possible. Otherwise planning undertaken by a Senior Management Team in touch with, and willing to address, the issues about which people are concerned, is satisfactory. By planning in this way schools are well prepared to take advantage of any government initiatives which carry additional funding as they come on stream.

But just as importantly they will most probably be doing a better job day by day for their gifted and talented pupils.

Planning at teacher level

Teachers who are supported by schools like those described above have a head start over teachers who are not. Nevertheless all teachers can help themselves to do a better job in whatever circumstances they are in if they have the will and the knowledge to do it.

The argument has just been put forward that schools need to plan for gifted and talented pupils specifically in order to get the best for them and do the best by them. This next section will focus on teacher planning as a somewhat obvious first step to doing the same thing at classroom level and thus improving the learning experiences of gifted and talented pupils. We will explain how teachers can plan at different levels to meet the individual needs of pupils and hopefully suggest some novel ways of obtaining information to facilitate effective planning.

Why plan?

In the first edition of this book (Clark and Callow 1998) we said, along with others, that planning is considered to be an essential aspect of effective and efficient teaching.

Pollard and Tann (1993) state that:

Planning is a highly skilled activity which at best requires a clear understanding of the curriculum; a consistent and appropriately resourced approach to learning which is school-wide; and teachers who are prepared to take into account in the planning pupil needs and interests.

Planning, however, discloses much more than what is to be taught.

A single lesson plan can provide a 'big picture of education':

- how teachers teach
- why they are teaching
- what they are teaching
- the way they are teaching it.

It gives insight into:

- how teachers think
- what is actually being taught
- the kinds of teaching and learning that are being experienced
- both the physical and social aspects of the learning environment.

The classroom practice which follows that plan reflects the personality, beliefs, values and assumptions of the teacher. Of course, pupils also affect what goes on in the classroom too but it is the teacher's stamp on the proceedings that leaves an indelible imprint.

Planning also makes explicit what otherwise might remain implicit because in order to plan teachers have to explain:

- what they intend to do
- why they are doing it
- how it is to be done
- how they intend to evaluate what they do.

Planning is therefore a highly professional activity. First-class planning where goals are set at the appropriate level should ensure that gifted and talented pupils have a satisfying learning experience.

This ought to limit underachievement and raise standards overall. First-class planning is a major step forward for gifted and talented pupils.

Understood from this perspective planning is a holistic activity which utilises the teacher's intellectual, cognitive, social and emotional energy. Genuine plans, not ones done merely as a paper exercise, tell us a great deal about teachers' perceptions of their role, how they facilitate learning, how they organise the learning experience and how they evaluate learning.

A plan, if it is genuine, is a personal statement about the educational context in which the teacher is working at classroom level, at school level, at cluster level, at local authority level, at national level and at international level.

Teachers are expected to focus on managerial, intellectual and cognitive aspects in their planning and as they work rather than on their feelings with regard to what they are doing. Feelings are often treated as an irrelevance to what goes on in the classroom when in fact they are central to what goes on. We see feelings as a touchstone to the emotional health of the teacher which should not be ignored. The emotional health of teachers can and should be sustained through professional development approaches such as the Integrated Approach.

Teacher planning therefore has a number of uses, each of which is valuable in a different way. These vary from the plan as a way of organising pupil learning to the plan as a way of gaining insight into teacher beliefs, values and assumptions.

There are also different sorts of plans which teachers are required to make. Research by Easen, Clark and Morrow (1993: 93) indicates that teachers do long-term, mid-term, short-term and daily planning. It was in daily planning that the greatest variation took place.

> Two predominant types emerged: one was comprehensive planning where a framework for future classroom action was specified and within which the daily plan was a rehearsal of what was intended to be taught; the second was a response to the dynamic interaction between teachers and learners and therefore largely dependent on the reaction of learners to the learning environment.

These plans were largely planned mentally and were an intensely personal response to the immediate. It is this kind of almost automatic response which requires closer analysis because of the insight it might well provide into the teacher's thoughts, feelings and beliefs. Such analysis results in increased self-awareness and understanding of the teaching and learning environment and this should enable teachers to match the learning experiences to pupil needs more accurately.

Planning in the classroom

Some of the different ways to elicit information to facilitate good planning are as follows.

a) Make use of mental planning processes

Mental planning informs daily planning. It happens at the interface of learning in an *ad hoc* fashion. It is very influential because unlike some forms of planning it affects directly what goes on in classrooms. Because it happens instinctively mental planning is often forgotten, which is a pity because it is important.

Suggestion

As soon after the lesson as possible, or indeed during the lesson if it is feasible, jot down a brief note of potentially important moments, that is moments that stand out in your mind as being of interest or importance.

Possible outcomes

These incidents might bring some influence to bear on the way you manage and organise things in the future.
   They could be used:

- to help with the evaluation of the lesson
- to provide specific information about individual learners
- to inform future planning

all in relation to gifted and talented learners in particular.

b) Teacher diaries

Writing a regular diary of events is another way of keeping track of what goes on in the classroom. If the diary includes accounts of what is said and what is done, it can provide information which can be analysed, interpreted and used to plan more accurately in the future.

Possible outcomes

Research by Clark (1993) found that diaries provided a starting point for teachers to take action.
   Teachers thought diary-writing helped them to come to terms with the emotional and psychological demands of teaching and learning. It also appeared to be a technique that facilitated self-development through what Grumet (1988) calls 'self-interpretation and self-determination'. Diaries can be analysed every week,

month or half-term to pick out trends and patterns. This can illuminate practice and suggest ways forward.

c) Observation

As documented in the last chapter observation has many uses and certainly the data can be used to inform planning.

Possible outcomes

The following could be used to analyse the data:

- What did the learners do which I intended?
- What did they do which I did not intend?
- To whom did they relate?
- What did they do when they were not on task?
- What kinds of things prevented them from getting on with the task?
  (Easen 1985)

This information can be used to facilitate planning that is more accurate, specific and appropriate for gifted and talented pupils.

Teacher planning is one of the most important activities a teacher does and it is vital that time is spent doing it in a way that is more than going through the motions to amass the necessary paperwork.

☞ **Informed planning is the key to differentiated learning which takes into account individual pupil needs.**

In relation to gifted and talented pupils in particular, higher order skills as described in Bloom's Taxonomy (1985) can be used to differentiate the curriculum. On a regular basis teachers should plan to ensure that gifted pupils are given the opportunity to:

- demonstrate their ability to translate; that is paraphrase, explain word meanings and select relevant information to answer questions;
- interpret by reordering facts, present a new view of material, compare and contrast and group or classify according to specified criteria;
- extrapolate, that is use data to determine consequences or effects, ascertain causes, implications, corollaries or results;
- apply ideas in different areas of study, utilise problem-solving techniques;
- transfer methods to new situations, bring new general principles to bear on new questions;
- analyse by breaking down the whole into constituent parts, differentiate between fact and hypothesis, identify hidden meanings, find themes or patterns, understand systems or organisations;
- synthesise through recombining elements to form a whole or to form a new statement, develop plans to test a new hypothesis, create a new form of classifying data, discover new relationships, invent or propose new alternatives

and attempt to change and improve ideas;
- evaluate by appraising, assessing and criticising on the basis of specific standards and demands by assessing work against recognised excellence;
- compare and discriminate between theories and generalisations and evaluate material according to specified criteria.

Bloom asserts that information-handling skills are the most important skills for gifted and talented pupils to acquire which is one of the reasons we have devoted an entire chapter to them.

There are many other ways to differentiate the curriculum for gifted and talented pupils which teachers can use when they are planning. These include:

Spillman's four approaches

Spillman (1991) provides in diagrammatic form (Figure 6.1) four ways in which activities can be organised:

- differentiation through work outcome
- differentiation through varied approaches to learning
- differentiation through varied stimuli
- differentiation through different tasks.

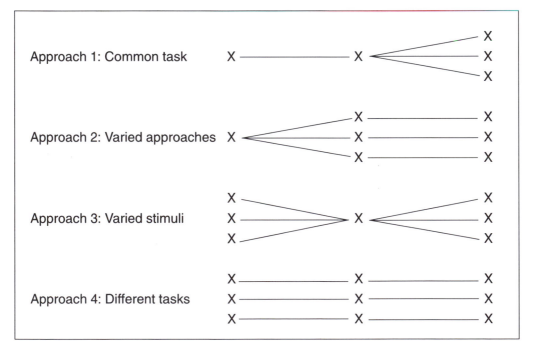

Figure 6.1 Spillman's four approaches

Barthorpe's optimum level

This is when all plans include an optimum level which aims to extend the learning of the brightest pupils. She suggests that gifted pupils are given a framework for a task with few cues in order to encourage hypothesis testing (Barthorpe 1994).

Making use of expert tutors

Appropriate curriculum differentiation can occur by using expert tutors to work with gifted pupils who enjoy working with someone who knows more about the subject than they do. Obviously tutors have to be carefully selected for suitability and checked out and they require guidance from the teacher about the work they are expected to do. They also need to be debriefed by the teacher following the lesson. Experts from universities, specialist colleges, the world of business and finance can all play a part.

Planning and evaluating for differentiation

Plans need to be manageable, concise and exact. The lesson concepts, skills and vocabulary should be clearly delineated on the plan alongside the questions to be asked.

The questions ought to be of different types to encourage different types of thinking.

The following questions can be useful for the purposes of evaluating and planning lessons for gifted and talented pupils (Table 6.1).

Table 6.1 A checklist for planning and evaluating the learning of gifted and talented pupils (Clark and Callow 1998)

A checklist for planning and evaluating learning

- What do I want to teach the children?
- Why do I want to teach it (other than because it is in the National Curriculum)?
- How do I intend to teach it?
  and
- Have I succeeded in teaching it?
- How do I know?
- What made the approach work for the gifted and talented pupils?
  or on the other hand
- Have I not succeeded in teaching it?
- How do I know?
- Why did the approach not work for the gifted and talented pupils?
- Where next?

Answers to these questions will result in feedback which will also feed forward to the next plan and go some way to 'matching' gifted and talented pupils with more appropriate learning experiences.

In conclusion

For planning to be effective it should be interrelated at school, key stage and classroom level. Classroom planning is a professional activity which at best not only ensures that teachers have an accurate action plan for effective teaching, but also provides insight into teacher thinking and practice, thus enhancing professional development. When techniques such as the analysis of mental planning, diary-writing or observation are used by teachers to inform planning, then the resulting professional development can positively affect the experiences of gifted and talented learners and indeed all learners, in classrooms and schools. The interlinking of planning and professional development will go a long way to ensure that gifted and talented children are being sufficiently challenged by their experiences in school.

References

Barthorpe, T. (1994) *Differentiation – Eight Ideas for the Classroom.* Scunthorpe: Desktop Publications.

Bloom, B. (1985) *Developing Talent in Young People.* New York, NY: Ballantine.

Clark, C. (1993) 'Changing teachers through telling stories', *Support for Learning* **8**(1), 31–4.

Clark, C. and Callow, R. (1998) *Educating Able Children: Resource Issues and Processes for Teachers.* London: David Fulton Publishers.

Easen, P. (1985) *Making School-centred INSET Work.* London: Croom Helm/Open University.

Easen, P., Clark, C. and Morrow, G. (1993) 'Teacher Planning and its Implications for Classroom Practice in the Primary School'. Paper prepared for the British Educational Research Association Annual Conference, Oxford.

Grumet, M. (1988) *Bitter Milk.* Amherst, MA: University of Massachusetts Press.

Her Majesty's Inspectorate (HMI) (1992) *The Education of Very Able Children in Maintained Schools.* London: HMSO.

Pollard, A. and Tann, S. (1993) *Reflective Teaching in the Primary School.* London: Cassell.

Roaf, C. and Bines, H. (eds) (1989) *Needs, Rights and Opportunities.* Lewes: Falmer Press.

Spillman, J. (1991) 'Decoding Differentiation', *Special Children* **44**, January, 7–10.

CHAPTER 7

Beginning to provide: resources for schools and teachers

This chapter is directed towards teachers and schools just beginning to provide for the needs of gifted and talented pupils. It will:

- offer help in formulating a pragmatic definition of the term 'gifted and talented';
- set out matters that should be considered in developing a scheme or school plan;
- look at organisational structures for provision;
- indicate resources, other than curriculum materials, available to the teacher.

Most probably one of the issues that teachers new to this field will confront immediately is the bewildering array of titles which have been used to describe the group of children we have called 'able' in the first edition of this book, including 'genius', 'gifted', 'clever', 'fast learners'. It must be accepted that there is no entirely satisfactory term. The DfES has adopted the phrase 'gifted and talented'. 'Gifted' refers to those with high ability or potential in academic subjects and 'talented' to those with high ability or potential in the expressive arts or sport (Ofsted 2001). While this designation is far from satisfactory on a number of counts, to save confusion it is used throughout this book.

A gifted and/or talented child will be good at something; it may be a particular academic subject such as mathematics, music or languages, or a group of subjects – perhaps mathematics, physics and biology. Or it may be that the child is a talented sportsperson, actor or dancer. Perhaps he/she shows great initiative and leadership qualities or a particular awareness and sensitivity to other people and issues of global concern such as poverty, pollution and famine. There is no homogeneous group which can be described as gifted and talented; rather, they are a disparate group. It is important to note that there are also some gifted and talented children who underachieve; who, for many reasons including lack of appropriate support from school and home, never do as well as they might have done. These children offer a particular challenge to their teachers. Whatever the ability, it can be identified, evaluated and challenged. Not all abilities are likely to be at the same level of development and a gifted and talented child may have other abilities which are nearer the average of his or her peers or even, on occasions, below them.

It is the belief of the authors that these abilities can be found in children of all races and classes, and that children, whatever their ability, are entitled to the best possible provision to meet their individual needs and develop their individual abilities. Furthermore, in a society like our own which actively promotes the abilities of sportsmen and women and musicians, we agree with Freeman (1998) that there should be no problem with the notion of advancing the case of the potential scientist, historian or philosopher based on the Sports Model of extra coaching; yet many teachers are strangely reluctant to accept this notion.

It may be useful at this point to identify two groups of gifted pupils. Broadly speaking, the first group are a recognisable band of high-ability pupils, probably two to four in an average mixed-ability class, representing about 10 per cent of the school population. Generally speaking, these children are likely to have an IQ of 120 or more on a test such as the Wechsler Intelligence Scale (WISC). This classification includes the 2 per cent of children generally accepted as 'gifted' who will have a much higher IQ than 120 (Callow 1994). Within this broad classification it is necessary to identify a very small group of children, perhaps one in ten thousand, of outstanding ability whom we call the 'exceptionally gifted', and who require a radically different form of educational provision (Gross 1993).

Since the majority of teachers are unlikely to encounter even one of these exceptionally gifted children in the course of their teaching careers, it is not our intention to do more than mention them here. A number of these exceptionally gifted children will attend specialist schools for music, dance or sport. However, the materials and methods outlined in this book can be adapted for use with the academically exceptionally gifted child, as we shall illustrate.

Perhaps the most important point is that teachers have no need to expend valuable time and energy in complex debates about definition. For practical purposes, the target group is that which the school or the individual teacher recognises as needing some distinctive provision. The following approaches are offered to assist schools in formulating an effective working definition.

Intelligence tests

It is possible to see different ability levels as sections of a normal distribution of ability. These can be equated with scores on any test that produces such a distribution.

Standardised tests are designed to compare a pupil's performance with that of others of a similar age. Such tests are devised so that the mean score is 100 and most have a standard deviation of 15 points, which means that just over two thirds of pupils obtain scores within the range 85 to 115. A normal distribution can be represented by Figure 7.1.

Unfortunately, an IQ score is not of much practical use to a teacher and may, on occasions, prove to be a handicap, since it gives little indication of the specific areas of a child's ability and may lead to the teacher having unrealistic expectations of

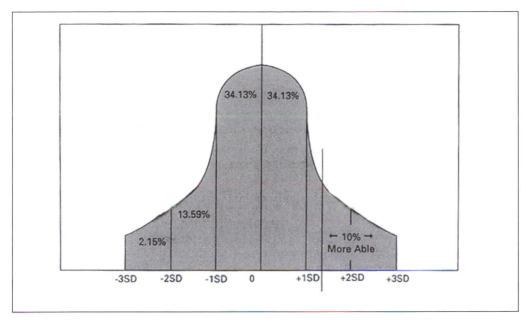

Figure 7.1 Intelligence: the normal curve

specific children. Having said this, in cases where, as a result of systematic teacher assessment over time, the teacher considers that a child may be gifted but is underachieving, an IQ test administered by a psychologist to provide evidence of general ability can act as a useful yardstick for both teacher and pupil to work with. Taken together with teacher assessment, the IQ score can be used in this way to raise the child's expectations as well as those of the teacher; in other words it can act as a motivator.

A test administered by a trained psychologist can show areas of strength and weakness, but these are only very general indications and are much more useful to the teacher of children with learning difficulties or emotional problems. The practical teacher is well advised to treat test results as one piece of evidence to be weighed carefully against all the other data available, not as a certificate of excellence or the opposite.

The checklist approach

The second approach is to regard high ability as defined by certain qualities, characteristics or skills. Three models are proposed for consideration. The first puts an emphasis on qualities. It suggests that it is not enough to find a quantitative hurdle for the gifted to leap over; instead there is something about the nature of that performance that goes beyond a simple test.

Qualities of the gifted

- excellence in performance relative to peers
- rarity
- beyond the average productivity – the quality yields something
- beyond the average demonstrability – the quality can be shown
- value – the quality is valued by society.

Another way forward is to look at the nature of 'ability' itself. It is possible to identify some key characteristics.

Key skills of the gifted

- speed of information processing
- highly efficient memory
- ability to see patterns and make connections
- intellectual curiosity.

The final example contains greater detail and includes characteristics that are more readily observable by the teacher.

Characteristics of the gifted

- to be capable of a high level of abstract thought
- to exhibit a high degree of curiosity
- to have a wide range of interests or hobbies
- to have an exceptional insight and depth of knowledge about interests and hobbies
- to be a good reader
- to learn easily and to be able to cope with complicated ideas or information
- to have a good vocabulary
- to be able to work independently for long periods at interesting and challenging tasks
- to be quick to respond to new or unusual ideas
- to have an original and lively imagination
- to be very mature socially
- to have a good sense of humour.

(Laycock 1957)

The categories approach

- general intellectual ability
- specific academic aptitude
- creative or productive thinking
- leadership qualities (social skills)
- visual and performing arts
- psychomotor ability.

(Marland Report 1972)

None of these approaches to definition – the test score, the checklist or the categories – is completely satisfactory on its own, but taken together they do offer useful insights into the nature of the gifted child and strongly suggest that it is necessary to keep an open mind and be aware of factors other than the successful performance of school tasks and assignments. High ability comes in different forms and there is not a single, simple benchmark.

It should also be apparent that many of the characteristics indicated depend upon perceptions of the child's actual performance on specific curriculum tasks. The sad fact is that much of the work children do in schools requires little intellectual effort, and success is more dependent upon obeying simple instructions and rote memory than on ability. Research done by Her Majesty's Inspectorate in the late 1970s revealed that there were few clues to secondary pupils' ability to be found in their workbooks because of the undemanding nature of the tasks presented (HMI 1979). The imposition of an overloaded and prescriptive National Curriculum has, in all probability, made this worse. It is important to understand that advanced abilities will only be manifested in response to challenging tasks which it is the responsibility of the class or subject teacher to provide.

Resources

It is axiomatic that the most valuable resources deployed in the classroom are the professional abilities of the teachers. Sadly, those teachers who remain in the profession have been systematically abused and denigrated over the last dozen years by the very politicians and government agencies that should have supported and encouraged them. They have been bombarded with unworkable ideas and burdened, like the White Knight, with a cumbersome and ever-changing set of curriculum requirements. It is our firm belief that teachers should be given the chance to deploy their very professional skills in the pursuit of education, not to be simply 'deliverers' of some fixed curriculum. (See Chapters 4, 5 and 6.)

Ideally, teachers must be sympathetic, perceptive, creative, mentally agile, and confident in their own abilities and skills. This confidence is particularly important when working with the gifted. Teachers often feel threatened by the idea of working with children potentially more advanced than themselves. But it must be remembered that teachers have maturity and experience on their side and, for these reasons, should remain in control of the organisation and planning, and the provision of suitable learning opportunities. However, teaching gifted children is bound to have implications for the pupil/teacher relationship. For instance, the older the children are, the more emphasis needs to be placed on shared learning and the seminar style of lesson management.

Identification and provision

To address successfully the issue of the gifted pupil, the teacher has to undertake two vital and interrelated tasks: firstly, to identify the gifted, however they are defined and, secondly, to provide for their educational needs. Generally speaking, if these tasks are not carried out successfully then the emotional and social needs of the pupil will not be satisfied. Of course, there are some high-ability children who have serious emotional and social problems caused by other factors than solely inappropriate schooling, just as there are high-ability children who have some form of physical handicap. But our aim is to focus on the group of gifted children, by far the largest, without such attendant problems, as these are the pupils teachers are more likely to encounter in the ordinary classroom setting. Having said this, some of the ideas suggested are adaptable for use with any pupil, including those with special educational needs.

Intelligently deployed, suitable and adequate resources can help teachers to perform both the task of identification and that of provision.

The teacher's role – general method

Infant teachers are well used to observing the way children tackle specific activities and talking to them to confirm the perceptions formed by observation. We need to employ similar methods to identify gifted and talented pupils across both phases, giving them challenging work to do, talking to them about it and evaluating their responses. (See Chapters 5 and 6.)

It will soon be discovered that certain pupils are good at solving problems of different types; some will produce unusual, ingenious solutions, others will be imaginative and yet others strictly logical in their approach to the task. Tasks can be introduced as supplementary work or small-group activities each day, and the work discussed with a few chosen children each day. This should take up no more than five or ten minutes of the teacher's time.

Start by using commercial materials and, when you are comfortable with them, you can perhaps devise problems of your own as class or group activities and introduce problem elements into the regular curriculum. This approach will allow the teacher to become familiar with the materials and identify the more effective activities. It is important that each child works at a variety of problems, practical, mathematical, literal and speculative (i.e. what would happen if . . .).

The following notes provide a summary of the teacher's approach to working with gifted and talented pupils.

The role of the teacher

Find lesson structures, materials and methodologies that encourage the pupils to:

- speculate and generate ideas with imagination and originality;
- expand their knowledge base and stretch their memories;
- question perceptively and demand logical responses from others;
- challenge accepted ideas and arguments;

- work independently, searching with confidence for meaning and pattern in abstract and concrete tasks;
- present ideas clearly and logically;
- gain experience in interpolation and extrapolation, deducing outcomes and making inferences.

Expect pupils to:

- work at a fast pace, assimilating and processing data rapidly and leaping stages in arguments and processes;
- handle multiple variables and adapt to new ideas and situations rapidly;
- make clear, precise, apposite responses to questions or tasks;
- produce work that is well presented, grammatical, accurate, rigorous;
- achieve an effective balance between selectivity and detail;
- evaluate their own work objectively and the work of others constructively;
- work cooperatively, accept valid criticism and respect the views of others.

Teachers should not be afraid to experiment with new ideas nor to abandon ruthlessly approaches that do not work. It is necessary to start slowly and gradually build up a bank of materials, ideas and strategies that work.

Above all, teachers must believe in what they are doing and be sympathetic and supportive to the children, carefully abstaining from sarcasm and mockery so that the classroom really is 'the safest place in the world to make a mistake' (Weber 1978).

The school

No teacher, however gifted, can hope to be really effective in isolation. His or her abilities will be best employed as part of a team working in a school that has a clear set of aims and objectives. For this reason, teachers' individual efforts will be deployed far more efficiently if the school has a written policy statement. This statement does not have to be very long or complex, but it should address the following matters:

- justification for action;
- definition of the target group;
- the process of identification;
- the process of provision;
- funding and the provision and storage of resources;
- strategies for introducing and developing the programme devised;
- overall responsibility for the programme;
- a timescale for implementation, review and revision;
- an investigation of available, published resources and an audit of resources already available within the school.

The first step should be the formation of a working party or planning group, chaired by a member of the Senior Management Team with responsibility for initiating and monitoring the programme.

Justification

It is important that any programme is firmly based on notions of fairness and equity, and that moral and philosophical implications are adequately discussed. For instance, some teachers may be unhappy at the idea of creating an elite who are in their opinion already sufficiently privileged and do not merit any additional resource or specialist provision. It is important, however, to remember that writing policies and setting up initiatives are practical matters and that time is of the essence. Of course, contentious issues should be aired and disagreements addressed but it is essential to agree on policy, planning and provision sooner rather than later. Any decisions made ought to be reviewed in the light of experience on an annual basis.

Definition of target group

Similarly, the issue of definition is one that should be discussed pragmatically as a practical curriculum-centred topic and not allowed to wander off in vague generalisations. The target group should be that which the teachers can easily identify as needing provision.

Identification procedures

Each school will have to establish a method of identifying their gifted and talented pupils. There are seven possible sources of evidence:

- tests and examinations
- the portfolio of evidence passed on from the previous school
- checklists
- National Curriculum level descriptors where useful
- teachers' perceptions
- parents' perceptions
- self-selection.

In devising a system for the identification of gifted children, it is important to accept that this is not a simple 'once and for all' process. No system is going to be 100 per cent accurate. Therefore it is necessary to reappraise the pupils on a regular basis and to review the system of identification regularly in the light of experience gained.

Portfolio from the previous school

It seems sensible to build on previous knowledge of individual pupils such as portfolios of evidence from previous schools. These can be a vital source of information. It is likely, though not absolutely certain, that gifted children will have already been identified, but the evidence from the portfolio should contain more than simple recognition. It has already been argued that identifying pupils on the basis of any single benchmark is insufficient. A standardised test may say one thing, a National Curriculum assessment another. Reports from the previous school may be different again. The portfolio approach enables schools to use a range of evidence in building up a balanced and informed picture of an individual child. In sifting through the evidence, the teacher can note comments as well as indicators which suggest a correlation with the definition points described in the previous section. In some cases all of these will point in one direction and the gifted child is easily identified, but in others the position will be less clear. Each child should be considered as an individual and recognition ought to be based on a weighing of all available evidence. The same principles apply when a child transfers from one secondary school to another as well as from primary to secondary school.

Checklists

A checklist is another way of helping teachers identify gifted pupils. While general abilities have a use in the early years of education when children's specific abilities are less clearly marked, they have to be used with caution. The list of characteristics shown below can be deployed for this purpose. Another more extensive general checklist follows.

A general abilities list

The gifted and talented pupil:

- concentrates attention and effort towards a specific goal or purpose
- subordinates lesser goals to the pursuit of the main goal
- is willing to work for long periods in pursuit of a specific goal
- is willing to challenge accepted ideas
- possesses intellectual rigour
- processes complex information swiftly
- spots inconsistencies in argument and gaps in knowledge
- jumps stages in reasoning
- recognises patterns and relationships
- generalises
- applies a general rule in specific circumstances
- applies ideas and techniques from separate disciplines in pursuit of an answer
- recognises and uses relevant items in a mass of data
- tests ideas and information critically
- generates valid ideas and hypotheses
- presents a logical argument and follows one to its conclusions
- assimilates and uses new ideas speedily
- summarises and articulates ideas and conclusions succinctly
- utilises a range of approaches to a difficult problem
- possesses an awareness of context
- has a good memory for general principles and specific detail.

This is an all-purpose list, but the process can be refined by looking more specifically at competencies in certain subjects. The procedure involves listing first the general abilities of the gifted pupil and then identifying the way they might be focused in a subject-specific context.

Schools can develop this procedure in all subject areas; here is an example.

A subject checklist for English at late primary or secondary level

The gifted child:

- is articulate;
- shows originality in writing;
- writes imaginatively;
- enjoys 'playing with words' and experimenting with 'new words';
- likes to read and discuss what has been read in depth with an adult or peer of the same or higher level of ability;
- demonstrates the ability to critique literature in terms of genre, the author's style of writing and the extent to which the author has achieved his/her goal;
- can put forward advanced arguments and counter-arguments with ease either orally or in writing;
- has read widely not only novels but plays, poems and literary essays.

These lists can be compiled by departments in secondary schools or at key stages in primary schools as a professional development exercise; it is a useful way to help colleagues clarify their views about what an able chemist, an able artist or whatever, might be expected to do.

An obvious way of using a checklist is to ask a teacher (or teachers) to put a tick, a cross or a question mark against each criterion for a particular pupil. This is better than using a number score which tends to complicate matters. This method is essentially criterion-driven. If the pupil displays the characteristic, it does not matter at this stage how well it is manifested. If teachers want to refine this approach, it is possible to use a double tick or a double cross to indicate degrees of certainty. There could also be a requirement to state, briefly, the evidence. It should be emphasised that no child is likely to fit all the criteria on the checklist and that a decision will, therefore, be taken on the overall weight of evidence. Any child meeting more than half the criteria in the general checklist is likely to fall into the category of 'gifted'.

A checklist or list of criteria, however good it is, can only be useful to the teacher if pupils can be observed using the abilities it identifies. Therefore, teachers need to ensure that pupils are given appropriate opportunities to display these qualities in day-to-day work with suitable curriculum materials.

A checklist or even a simpler list of specific aptitudes and abilities can be used directly in the identification process or to generate test items or tasks. Wherever possible, teachers should endeavour to discuss the completed tasks with the children to obtain the fullest information about their abilities and thus inform their judgements.

An example of a checklist devised to appraise individual project work is given below:

- vocabulary and use of words
- analysis, evaluation, judgement
- conceptual understanding
- logic and rigour in reasoning
- synthesis of complex ideas
- reading level required by sources
- confidence
- commitment to the task

The work could also be vetted by reference to the level descriptors in the National Curriculum. It will be noted that once again recognition does not involve demanding perfection. That Holy Grail eludes even gifted and talented pupils!

Provision and implementation

Among other matters, then, the working party will have addressed the following issues in very general terms:

- identification of the target group
- the process of identification
- the process of provision
- finding and storage of resources
- strategies for developing the programme
- overall responsibility for implementation and a timetable for implementation.

The next task will be to make the general guidelines more specific and ensure that progress in provision and implementation really occurs. There should be four strands to any implementation programme:

1. The introduction of specific curriculum materials and activities into the everyday timetabled work of the school.
2. The development of extra-curricular activities.
3. The inservice training of the staff.
4. The evaluation of specific materials and methods and the overall effectiveness of the whole programme.

How responsibility for the management of these elements is allocated will depend to a large extent on the size of the school. In a small primary school one experienced teacher can cope with all four areas; in a large comprehensive school, however, the work could well be divided between several staff members.

As the members of staff become accustomed to the materials, and become aware of the best ways of deploying them, some of them will see how the content could be improved and realise the need to extend its scope. This is an important stage since the very best materials can be those devised by teachers themselves in a writing group. This can take many forms, which might involve:

- a group, or groups, of teachers drawn from several schools, preferably under the guidance of a local authority adviser/inspector;
- a group of teachers from a single school;
- a single department in a comprehensive school, working within their own discipline;
- a cluster of departments working on a cross-disciplinary theme.

However groups are constituted, the following guidelines should be helpful:

- The leader of the group should have a relatively high status, e.g. head teacher, adviser, head of department.
- The members should be volunteers.
- The leader should be free to organise the group to encourage the maximum productivity. Some teachers are naturally creative and will produce a wealth of ideas, while others less creative may have the ability to develop an idea or the persistence to turn it into an effective unit of work. It is the group leader's responsibility tactfully to guide each member into the role where they will be most effective and gain the maximum satisfaction from their work.

The course of the sessions should take this form:

- Selection of area of interest.
- Survey and evaluation of existing materials.
- Definition of area for development.
- Brainstorming session.
- Writing preliminary draft materials, which are copied and disseminated to all members of the group.
- Discussion and possible revision of materials.
- Evaluation in school.
- Summary of evaluation.
- Further revision and evaluation if necessary. Groups should not be disappointed if their first attempts need revision; the process of writing, evaluating and revising is the important element.
- When a suitable body of materials is produced it can be widely disseminated. Where clusters of groups exist they can exchange materials for trial and evaluation. If the local authority has a resources unit, the best materials can be printed and promoted commercially to other authorities.
- The group, under the guidance of their leader, must keep a firm perception of

the original objectives. If necessary, 'experts' from other disciplines or from other institutions may need to be consulted, but their enthusiasm or views, while of value, should not be allowed to divert or derail the course of the original programme.

Working with parents

Parents are in a position to know their own child better than anyone else. Although they cannot be completely objective, and are not necessarily in a position that allows them to compare their own child with its peers, their opinion should be taken seriously. They can be an additional resource to the teacher as well as to their own child, and therefore, for all concerned, it is important that the school establishes a good relationship with parents as early as possible. In some schools as soon as the gifted and talented pupils have been identified, parents are invited to school to meet the year head and either the Key Stage Coordinator or the Key Person with responsibility for gifted and talented pupils. At the interview, the teachers share with parents what the identification process has indicated and explain what the school intends to do during the forthcoming academic year in order to provide an appropriate curriculum experience. At the same time they discuss ways in which the parents can play a part in ensuring that their child will achieve what is expected of them. Sometimes parents are encouraged to complete a short questionnaire about their child which, taken together with a questionnaire completed by the child him/herself, can provide a fuller picture of what, for instance, they like best about school, what their hobbies are and so on. It might also be an idea to involve the child in the interview, or at least part of it, so that everyone involved is clear about what is happening and should happen in the future (Leroux and McMillan 1993, George 1992).

Something to bear in mind is that the gifted often perform well below the level their ability warrants if they are bored or working in an uncongenial atmosphere. Every effort should be made to determine areas in which the parents feel that their child is insufficiently challenged, in case this is happening. The child should then be given an opportunity to prove him/herself against more challenging tasks and the results carefully evaluated. Certainly no parents' ideas should be brushed aside without a sympathetic hearing and a close examination of the facts.

Another possibility is the compilation of a handbook of ways in which parents can work with, encourage and support their gifted child to achieve appropriately. Handbooks that are written through collaborative endeavour – for instance, between the parent of a gifted and talented pupil, the Key Person and possibly another senior manager – are usually more user-friendly and useful than ones written by the Key Person alone. A helpful way forward for schools considering such a handbook is to use a question-and-answer format of 'typical questions' from a parent: for example, 'Whom do I approach in school if I think my child is gifted?' or 'How can I help my child?' Another useful hint is to provide a draft copy of the handbook for a small number of parents of gifted children and teachers who have a known interest in the gifted to obtain their views about the handbook and use their comments to modify it before it is more widely dispersed.

Partnership with parents

The work of the school can be immeasurably assisted by the cooperation and insight of the children's parents, and it is important that the professionals do all that they can to involve them in the educational process.

When any special initiative, group or Saturday morning class is planned, the parents should be kept fully informed and their help and cooperation welcomed. Where they have valid reasons for concern, they should be given serious, courteous attention. Each school will doubtless establish its own system for informing parents and hearing their concerns.

Experience over 30 years of counselling the parents of gifted and exceptionally gifted children has led me to the following conclusions. The vast majority of parents are happy to cooperate with the school and be realistic about their own child. There are, however, two small groups who cause most of the concern, and they are those who have misguided expectations of their offspring's ability, and others who are working towards their own private agenda.

An example of the first type might be authoritarian parents, who believe that school is 'soft' and that they know better. They will often subject their luckless child to endless pages of repetitive 'homework', using some of the over-priced 'progress' papers to be found in any chainstore bookshop. They will expect their child to be reading books far beyond their interest level, or reach levels of calligraphy only attainable by third year art undergraduates. They will have been immeasurably helped in their beliefs by the arrant nonsense about 'standards' which passes for educational debate among politicians and other members of Islington's chattering classes.

The second, quite tiny, group consists of those whose child is either failing within the system or has behavioural problems. Parents are unwilling to blame themselves or their child-rearing practices, and search for an excuse. Often they run the gamut of fashionable reasons – 'He's dyslexic', 'She is dyspraxic' and often, when all else fails, 'She is very gifted.' This implies that the child is not like other mortals and is bored and confined within the cruel state system. There is much literature from the experts which can be used to confirm them in this belief.

Where any parent is concerned about their child's progress, the school must listen and take active steps to determine how far the concerns expressed are valid. Many troublesome children do have high ability and schools do misjudge pupils' ability.

The children should be given every chance to show their ability with process-based tasks; their performance should be carefully observed and recorded and related to the performance of the peer group. In areas of doubt the school's psychological service can help by indicating any area where a child has advanced ability. Where the parents' assessment of the child's ability is shown to be fairly accurate, there should be no problem in putting matters right. In every case the parents must be made aware of the purposes of the materials in use and shown how their child has performed, and have the implications of this explained.

Where a child has ability but is being burdened with unsuitable expectations and repetitive tasks, attempts should be made to divert the parents' efforts into more productive activities. Explain to them that they can help their child best by:

- massively supporting any worthwhile interest the child expresses;
- encouraging the fullest use of the public library system for factual and reference material, as well as for fiction;
- encouraging visits to museums and art galleries;
- planning visits to places of cultural interest rather than funfairs or 'theme parks';
- buying suitable computer programs.

For very young children especially:

- reading with the child and discussing the story;
- talking to the child as much as possible;
- encouraging the development of vocabulary: 'Can you hear the leaves rustling?'
- answering their questions: 'You should hold on tightly because if the bus stops suddenly you will be thrown forward very hard by its momentum'; 'Momentum is . . .';
- asking questions of your own: 'Why do you think that piece floats and that piece sinks?';
- trying to provide toys that will give scope for imaginative play and encourage coordination and spatial perception, tactical thinking and interest, e.g. jigsaws, blocks, farm animals, draughts, chess, etc.

Coping with these two groups of parents is very time-consuming and the school can be greatly helped if the local authority has an adviser or advisory teacher for gifted and talented pupils. Children of High Intelligence (CHI) and the National Association for Gifted Children (NAGC) also offer a counselling service in some parts of the country, and it might be possible to enlist their help – but only in the last resort and only if you are sure that the counsellors share the school's view.

In the last analysis, however, one has to accept that not every parent will come to agree with what is being done or proposed, and that some will go their own way whatever is done or said.

Self-selection

Teachers may be uncomfortable with the idea of letting gifted and talented pupils choose themselves, but it can be appropriate in certain circumstances. For example, a voluntary activity may allow pupils to come forward and in effect nominate themselves for participation. If the activity is not suitable for them, they will quickly find out and abandon it. This is not always satisfactory, as the more easy-going or 'hidden' gifted pupil may not come forward, but it should be noted that this is put forward only as one possible form of identification. It does, of course, acknowledge the importance of motivation. But it is always worthwhile to give pupils a chance to prove themselves if this can be done without a great deal of administrative labour.

Lack of pupil motivation presents a difficult problem. However, a school that offers a range of club activities, and extra school visits and activities, and organises timetable suspension events, where the children are allowed to choose activities, stands a better chance of identifying poorly motivated pupils. Careful monitoring of performance and informal discussions following such activities will often reveal surprising abilities in some pupils.

Structuring the provision

The next area the working party will need to discuss is the organisational arrangements necessary to meet the needs of gifted and talented pupils. It is an underlying assumption of this book that these needs will be catered for in ordinary classes as part of normal curriculum arrangements, and the next section on learning opportunities is written with this in mind: Consideration is given to whole-class organisation, the specific point of acceleration, and opportunities beyond the timetabled curriculum.

Schools may find it helpful to consider the following broad categories of organisation:

- working within the normal timetabled curriculum
- extended curriculum activities
- resources and opportunities beyond the school itself.

Although, as stated above, the needs of gifted and talented children will be met predominantly in what schools provide as part of their normal arrangements, there are other possibilities and these should be examined as a means of enriching what is available. Nevertheless, it must be recognised that there are practical issues involved in structuring arrangements for gifted and talented pupils. They concern the content, resources and methodologies used in lessons. There is also the matter of feelings and attitudes. Gifted children, if they are few in number, may feel isolated. They may need assurance that they are not alone, even that their interests are valid and that their high ability is to be encouraged. At the same time young people have a natural affinity with their own age group and indeed can learn from contact with those of differing abilities. The best approach is to achieve a balance between these two demands; on the one hand, opportunities for the 'congregation' of the able and, on the other, location within the peer group.

Streaming, setting and banding

A pragmatic and flexible approach is recommended for all pupils including the gifted (DfEE 1998). Streaming has generally been discarded as a rather too inflexible arrangement, though more broadly based banding systems are becoming increasingly popular as a way of working on raising standards of achievement for all pupils, based on the principle that children who are roughly of the same standard motivate each other to achieve. However, it is unlikely that a band can be defined to be coterminous with the category of gifted pupils and certainly not those of the exceptionally and very gifted. It follows that even in banding arrangements their needs are met in a broader context. Another approach is one that some teachers consider to be even more manageable than banding: that is to teach children of approximately the same standard in sets. There is some evidence which indicates that gifted children do better academically when they work with other gifted children (Robinson 1991, Kulik 1992, Whitty, Edwards and Power 1998). Setting can allow for finer tuning in relation to ability, especially when specific subject criteria are used for the purpose of set selection. It recognises that subjects require different teaching-learning strategies and that pupils have ability profiles. It also simplifies the arrangements for differentiation: however, it does not guarantee differentiation. Subject departments need to consider the programmes of work and targets for different sets with care to ensure that the rationale for setting is justified. Even within a top set, gifted and talented pupils can remain unchallenged and under-extended.

Mixed-ability arrangements are often included as a matter of policy for some subjects and younger year groups, and as a matter of necessity for some Key Stage 4 options. There is no reason why gifted children should not thrive in mixed-ability classes, but teachers need to be imaginative about how they implement strategies for differentiation. There are also broader educational and social arguments for letting children work some of the time with a heterogeneous group of peers. It would appear that, for instance, working in mixed-ability groups enhances the social development of gifted pupils (Tann 1988).

The conclusion to this discussion must be that the schools have to be pragmatic in their arrangements. There is no one method of organisation that works in all circumstances and meets every need. It is also the case that organisation is often constrained by administrative factors. The safest thing is to realise that organisation on its own does not provide for gifted and talented pupils. Nevertheless it is crucial that the rationale for any form of organisation is discussed, fully understood and agreed by all staff so that a consistent approach exists throughout the school.

Acceleration

The principle of acceleration suggests organisational strategies that allow children to work on advanced programmes or alongside those much older than themselves.

There have been cases of exceptionally gifted pupils progressing to GCSE, and GCE 'A' level and beyond, years ahead of the expected age, and there is often pressure for them to do that. These are likely to be rare, and even here there may be social and emotional problems and a question of what the accelerated learning actually leads to. All children, even gifted children, are entitled to a childhood (or an adolescence). Schools are advised to seek specialist external guidance with regard to promotions beyond the chronological age, especially if this is by more than one year group.

There are some possible compromises. A modified form of promotion is to teach a child in the age-appropriate class or year group, while allowing placement in an older class or group for certain periods. This is obviously likely to create timetable difficulties, but there are occasions when it may be feasible. Another is to create specific occasions when groups of pupils can associate with older persons (pupils or even adults), particularly if the peer group does not provide sufficient mental stimulus. This may occur in tutor groups, through personal and social education or in extra-curricular activities. It recognises that sometimes gifted children are frustrated because they have limited opportunities to communicate at the level of intellectual maturity of which they are capable. Schools do not always show sufficient awareness of this problem, though in some practical activities (for example, a school play) they may actually be tackling it.

Also some schools, secondary schools particularly, use teachers as mentors for their gifted and talented pupils. This appears to work best if the child chooses a teacher they like as their mentor. The mentoring sessions provide the children with the opportunity to discuss anything they wish, including, of course, their school work. For example, some pupils seek help with study skills, others wish to discuss the pressures that can result from being gifted, and others want specific advice about courses in higher education and career possibilities.

Another alternative to acceleration is the express class. These are specifically allowed under National Curriculum arrangements, particularly in facilitating early entry for GCSE. For most schools the express class has to be integrated into the standard school structure – in other words, a group that takes an examination in Year 10 still has to be catered for in Year 11. This requires very careful planning so that express class pupils do not feel they are standing still in Year 11 or indeed in the years following. Some secondary schools, for example, with their very brightest pupils in the sixth form start university courses to keep levels of motivation high. Among universities that are pioneering this approach are Newcastle University and the Open University.

In the primary school setting there is no reason why gifted children should not be working a key stage ahead of their peers. Again, careful consideration has to be given to what happens if this goes on throughout their primary schooling: will there come a point when they feel that they are marking time? Or would it be possible to work on the secondary school syllabus in the primary school with the help of colleagues from the secondary school? Or, indeed, should early secondary transfer be considered?

Where a school identifies a child of exceptional ability, some form of acceleration offers the best organisational response to his or her needs, and it may well involve early admission to the secondary phase or part-time attendance at a secondary or tertiary institution. Any radical acceleration must be systematically planned and monitored once it happens. It should only be undertaken after very thorough consultation with all the agencies involved, the child's parents and also the child him/herself. The rule of thumb is that if acceleration, and most certainly radical acceleration, is to be successful, then the child has to want this to happen and needs to be mature in all aspects of development, that is socially, emotionally and physically as well as intellectually (Hymer and Harbron 1998).

Beyond the timetabled curriculum

Special arrangements can be made for gifted and talented pupils through extra-curricular activities organised by the school. There are also opportunities created by other agencies which deserve consideration.

Extra-curricular activities

- school clubs and interest groups;
- 'twilight' special classes, across a year group, across a phase or part of a phase, in one school or a cluster;
- suspension of timetable for a day or half-day for groups to follow a variety of activities;
- partial suspension of the timetable for individual children to follow chosen projects under the guidance of school tutors;
- seminars and workshops with visiting experts, e.g. artists, musicians;
- Saturday morning classes;
- focused visits to theatres, galleries, museums;
- special courses at colleges and universities for groups or individuals;
- Open University courses – it is now possible for young people to get accreditation for courses followed;
- attendance at specific lectures or series of lectures at a college or university;
- summer schools.

Schools should not be afraid to use the extended curriculum as the basis for organising activities. It is as legitimate to organise a club or a special event, with intellectual content likely to attract the academically gifted, as it is to establish teams and competitions likely to attract those with sporting prowess. Most schools have teachers whose own interests and talents can be exploited in this way. This is the Sports Model, as advocated by Freeman (1998), which emphasises that appropriate and regular coaching similar to that offered to those talented in sport should be available to those with other gifts and talents. Freeman advocates coaching for the academically gifted to enhance their skills.

Some schools organise cluster or pyramid out-of-school sessions for their gifted and talented pupils, which utilise the expertise of volunteer staff from the schools to provide challenging experiences. Often these are of a problem-solving nature. Some of the best problems are 'real problems', that is problems identified by the children; for instance, something about their school they would like to change which will have an effect on their lives.

There are also, of course, resources outside the school, which can act as a broker in bringing pupils in contact with a wide range of interests and opportunities. One of the most frequently used forms of extra-curricular provision is the Saturday morning class. It can take a number of forms. At its simplest it involves a group of children meeting at a school or hall to pursue one or more activities, organised by volunteers, during the course of a Saturday morning, with a small charge made to cover the costs of the premises and refreshment. It may be a single event or part of a series, organised by a group like CHI or the NAGC or by a local authority.

Benefits of special arrangements

- There is great flexibility. Numbers can be as small or as large as desired. It presents an option accessible to the largest LEA and the smallest primary school.
- Organisation is simpler because it takes place outside normal timetable constraints.
- Pupils and teachers work in a more relaxed atmosphere. Smaller groups permit ideas to be challenged and discussed more readily.
- Teachers experiment and develop teaching ideas and strategies. Materials piloted there can be later refined for classroom use.
- Secondary schools have an opportunity to work with and assess the gifted children in feeder primaries.
- Pupils have an opportunity for new experiences and learning and a chance to grow intellectually.
- Pupils have contact with the wider world, with enthusiasts, local experts, college and university lecturers and business people.

But there are issues to be addressed if this way forward is envisaged. There is a need for clear, fair criteria for the selection of pupils for these sessions which are accepted by all involved. It is also preferable for there to be progression in work from session to session so that a topic can be developed over time. Furthermore, if adults who are not currently employed as teachers are to be involved, they need to be vetted before being allowed to work with the children, and this includes a police check.

Physical resources

Some materials have been specially produced for gifted and talented pupils and we will provide you with as full a list as we can. It is important to stress, however, that books and work units currently being utilised in classrooms will form the basis of the available resources for the gifted and talented pupils. Textbooks, tasks, topics and worksheets will all have to be modified and developed by the teachers themselves to fit the purposes of educating these pupils appropriately. Consequently, while the materials we mention in this book will be very useful, of much greater importance are the processes and methods we describe, which can be used to inform the ways the teacher uses materials, even materials not specifically designed for the gifted. Suffice to say that every scheme of work, indeed every lesson plan, should have a section on differentiation for the gifted or talented child.

Beyond the school

With a school plan in place, the resources available within the wider community should be explored. Some local education authorities employ advisers or advisory teachers with a responsibility for gifted and talented children, and specialist advisers can often offer invaluable help and advice, as can the local Education Resource Centre if one still exists.

One extremely valuable source of materials and expertise is the library service, which is often underused by schools, and steps should be taken to investigate the range of resources and support that is available. Another possibility is to invite professional writers, artists, musicians and crafts-people to be in residence in the school for a term (through bodies such as the Arts Council) to provide support and challenge for all the pupils, but especially children who are talented in these fields. Another useful idea is to make use of theatre, ballet and opera companies on tour, who often have an educational programme ongoing and are prepared to come and work in schools.

Many universities also offer courses and materials for gifted and talented pupils in specific subject areas, particularly science and maths. Teacher training institutions can sometimes provide groups of students who can work with a school on particular projects over a period of a term or more. It is both reassuring and challenging for gifted and talented children to have educational experiences of this kind, especially when they work within such a tightly prescribed curriculum day by day.

Art galleries and museums not only offer places to visit but can provide additional sources of expertise and knowledge, and there is much to be gained from approaching local clubs and societies. To give an example from our own recent experience, an authority-wide enrichment initiative in Merseyside was generously supported by two universities, a college of education, the museum service, and a host of hobby clubs, including ship modellers and war-gamers.

Initiatives beyond the school are very important, but of equal if not more importance, as will be seen in the next chapters, is what happens on a daily basis for gifted and talented pupils.

Some of the organisations that have a specific concern for gifted and talented children are listed in Appendix 1. They can in no way be seen to be rivals.

References

Callow, R. (1994) 'Classroom provision for the able and exceptionally able child', *Support for Learning* **9**(4), 151–4.

Department for Education and Employment (DfEE) (1998) *Excellence in Schools.* London: The Stationery Office.

Freeman, J. (1998) *Educating the Very Able: Current International Research.* London: HMSO.

George, D. (1992) *The Challenge of the Able Child.* London: David Fulton Publishers.

Gross, J. (1993) *Exceptionally Gifted Children.* London: Routledge and Kegan Paul.

Her Majesty's Inspectorate (HMI) (1979) *Aspects of Secondary Education in England and Wales.* London: HMSO.

Hymer, B. and Harbron, N. (1998) 'Early Transfer: a good move?', *Educating Able Children*, Spring, 38–48.

Kulik, J. (1992) *An Analysis of the Research on Ability Grouping.* Connecticut: University of Connecticut National Research Center on the Gifted and Talented.

Laycock, S. R. (1957) *Gifted Children: A Handbook for the Classroom Teacher.* Toronto: Copp-Clark.

Leroux, J. and McMillan, E. (1993) *Smart Teaching – Nurturing Talent in the Classroom and Beyond.* Markham, Ontario: Pembroke Publishers.

Marland, S. P. (1972) 'Education of the Gifted and Talented'. Report to Congress by the US Commissioner for Education. Washington DC: US Office of Education.

Office for Standards in Education (Ofsted) (2001) *Providing for Gifted and Talented Pupils: An Evaluation of Excellence in Cities and Other Grant-funded Programmes.* London: The Stationery Office.

Robinson, A. (1991) *Cooperative Learning and the Academically Talented Student.* Connecticut: University of Connecticut National Research Center on the Gifted and Talented.

Tann, S. (1998) 'Grouping and the Integrated Classroom', in Thomas, G. and Feiler, A. (eds) *Planning for Special Needs.* Oxford: Blackwell.

Weber, K. J. (1978) *Yes They Can!* Milton Keynes: Open University Press.

Whitty, G., Edwards, A. D. and Power, S. (1998) *Destined for Success? Educational Biographies of Academically Able Pupils.* Swindon: Economic and Social Research Council.

CHAPTER 8

Information handling as a resource

The process curriculum

There is an increasing tendency in schools currently to think of the curriculum solely as a matter of teaching content: it may be tables in mathematics, facts about a historical character or products exported from a certain foreign country. But this is nothing new, as schools traditionally have been places where such things have been considered of great importance. While the acquisition of a knowledge base is of course essential, and in some cases basic to the educational process (tables in mathematics are a case in point), another element is of equal importance – the development of necessary intellectual skills. Facts by themselves are of little account unless we give children an opportunity to acquire the necessary skills and attitudes to use those facts in a constructive and meaningful way. Unless we allow the children to develop their critical faculties, to think deeply, to speculate and to experiment with ideas, the knowledge they acquire will be largely meaningless.

Three processes appear to be necessary in varying degrees for the successful pursuit of any subject, whether in school or out. These are:

- information handling
- problem solving and creative thinking
- communication skills.

These processes are not the sole preserve of the gifted and talented. All children should be given access to them – few ever are. Materials that require the child to employ these processes will serve two functions. Firstly, they will help the teacher to identify the child who is capable of sustained intellectual effort and, secondly, they will provide some of the necessary curriculum content for that child's educational growth (Callow 1997).

Children are growing up in a society that is, more than any other, dependent upon the swift transmission and evaluation of information. Without access to the necessary skills for retrieving and processing information, a child will be severely handicapped in the modern world. Yet these skills are rarely systematically taught in schools. This chapter aims to set out some of the basic elements in this process and to indicate how they might be developed. It might be argued that the rapid development of electronic information technology has rendered these notions obsolete, but the basic skills are actually more vitally needed as technology develops, and there is no substitute for the written word – however transmitted.

Information-handling skills

Consequently, in almost any subject the skills of handling information are of great importance. What is illustrated below is a hierarchy of skills, showing how each demands higher order competences of gifted children.

1. Identification of a topic within a field of study and a general search of source materials.
2. Selection of a profitable line of enquiry, and narrowing of focus of source materials with more specific reading.
3. Hypothesis production.
4. Analysis – selection of specific pieces of information, data and argument; putting both sides of the argument.
5. Synthesis – construction of a coherent text from the separate elements.
6. Judgement – consideration of worth of text on grounds of

   - presentation
   - coherence
   - relevance and validity of argument
   - proof or otherwise of hypothesis.

7. Selection of new line of enquiry springing from the completed work.

It is possible to analyse each of these stages into a number of processes, which can be taught and evaluated in discussion with the pupil.

The skills and processes necessary for information handling

Skills	Processes
1. Defining objectives	(a) identifying area of search
	(b) formulating general questions
	(c) evaluating existing knowledge
	(d) formulating tentative hypotheses
	(e) considering time available.
2. Selection skills	(a) selection of relevant information
	(b) appraising information
	(c) deciding if information is sufficient for one's purposes

        (d) selection of correct reading mode, e.g. scanning or skimming

        (e) selection of appropriate questions

        (f) identifying main ideas.

3. Hypothesis production

        (a) organising ideas

        (b) selecting main elements or concepts

        (c) openness to new ideas and information

        (d) seeing arguments from different aspects

        (e) judgement of validity of ideas or concepts

        (f) identifying weak links in chain of reason

        (g) emotional detachment from subject.

4. Locating information (analytical process)

        (a) using books: alphabetical order; use of contents page; use of references and indices; use of glossary

        (b) using the library: finding the right books; using classification system; index or computer database; microfilm and microfiche; using library loan service

        (c) retrieval from electronic systems, e.g. Internet

        (d) transactional reading; reading carefully, checking for understanding and rereading, interrogating a sentence or paragraph

        (e) note taking

        (f) developing own reference system

        (g) interpretation of pictures, maps, artefacts, buildings, plans and diagrams.

5. Organising information

        (a) by forming concepts and generalisations

        (b) by rational and systematic study

        (c) by careful note taking

        (d) by arranging ideas in sequence

        (e) by summarising main points.

6. Evaluating information

        (a) by understanding implications

        (b) by relating to other knowledge already gained

        (c) by distinguishing fact and opinion, assessing accuracy of source – amount of bias/propaganda

        (d) by comparing with information from other sources

        (e) by establishing authority of information, date, author, etc.

If these skills and processes are systematically developed, the gifted child, in the later years of even the primary phase, should be able to identify, plan and research specific topics with only minimal input from the teacher.

Sources of information

1. Books, including reference and information works, and fiction where useful
2. Magazine articles, e.g. *National Geographic, Scientific American, Astronomy*
3. Newspaper articles and reports
4. Microfilm material
5. Computer material, e.g. Encarta, Internet material
6. Primary sources, first-hand interviews and archive material: letters, records, parish registers, bills and account books
7. Pictorial materials, graphs, diagrams, plans, maps, photographs and paintings
8. Film and sound tape
9. Buildings: castles, churches, etc.
10. Artefacts: furniture, clothing, weapons, etc.
11. Archaeological and historical sites, e.g. Jorvik, Bosworth battlefield complex.

Making a start

Books

An audit should be made of the books in the school and class libraries to find out what information books are available in the main curriculum areas – particularly history, RE, geography and science. It is amazing how many resources disappear over the years into cupboards, or onto obscure shelves, to be used perfunctorily or forgotten. Some topics will possibly be found to be well covered – they may be dinosaurs, transport or the Romans – and these could form the nucleus of the first topic collections. One or two topics can be assigned to each year group to avoid the duplication reported in Chapter 5. Clearly the subject matter and reading level of the materials will be taken into account when undertaking this task.

The topic collections should be clearly colour-coded and placed in the school topic library. As funds allow, decisions can be made about augmenting existing topic sets and buying materials to increase the number of topics available. Contact children's librarians and Teacher Resource Centres (if they exist) to find out about the range of materials they have available to complement the school's existing resources. It is important to stress that teachers should monitor the quality of any materials acquired. Bookshops are full of brightly coloured, attractive information books which many teachers rush to buy without critical examination. Before you set out to spend the yearly book allowance it is important to think about the sort of books that will be of most use, and ask a number of questions.

(a) Do you need an expensive encyclopaedia or books on specific subjects?
(b) Is it more cost-effective to buy one or two expensive texts or a greater number of cheaper ones?

When considering a particular book, take into account the following:

- Is the reading level suitable for the children?
- Does it have a clear, accurate text?
- Are the illustrations clear and accurate, and complementary to the text?
- Is there a contents page?
- Is there an accurate and full index?
- Is there a glossary?
- Does it cover those areas that you want covered, or will you need a second complementary text?
- Is the book attractively produced and easy for a child to handle?

Progress in information handling

Work on information skills can start before a child can read.

At infant level
The teacher can initially ask questions based on a picture or series of pictures, from illustrated books of an appropriate level, even strip cartoons such as Asterix or Tintin.

Example
Looking at a picture of a family having a picnic by a riverside.

Level 1: Analysis
Simple literal questions:
'What colour is Susan's dress?'
'What is Peter handing to his father?'

Level 2: Synthesis
Questions that require the child to pick up a number of visual clues:
'What time of year is it?'
'Why did they choose this place for a picnic?'

Level 3: Judgement
Questions involving the child's imagination and interest:
'Do you like picnics?'
'What do you think they will do after tea?'
'What is Susan thinking?'

Level 4: Further investigations

At lower junior level

When starting with written responses, it might be helpful for the child to be required simply to fill in a single word or phrase. As the child's competence and confidence grows, a whole sentence or short paragraph might be required. At this stage the children will benefit from clear and simple instructions which can form part of an individual work card, which the teacher has constructed as part of a carefully graded series.

Example
Card A5
Go to the library and look for a book called *Cavemen to Vikings* by R. J. Unstead (1974). You will find it in the history section. Go to the contents page at the front of the book and find the chapter 'The Early Cavemen'. Read the chapter and answer these questions:

Level 1: Analysis
'What kinds of food did the cave people eat?'
'What kinds of things did they make from flint?'

Level 2: Synthesis
'Why did early people choose to live in caves?'
(The child would have to assemble the answer from the text and make inference from references to the weather and to danger from predators.)
'Why was fire so important to the cave people?'
(The child is required to deduce uses from references to weather and predators as above – and from references to cooking and cave paintings.)

Level 3: Judgement
'How can the author be sure that the cavemen painted the pictures?'
'Would you like to have lived in the Stone Age?'
'Why did the cave people paint pictures?'

Level 4: Further investigations
'What would you like to know about the cave people which the book does not tell you?'

It cannot be stressed too strongly that the teacher must control the resource material to ensure that the child has access to all the information required and that it is available in a clear understandable form; also that the child is given help in finding where that information is. Practice can be given in finding and following up references and in collating the information gathered from a number of reference sources.

As children gain in confidence and skill, they can be required to use more than a single source and to write short articles on each topic. There are many ways of organising such work – as group or individual activities, with a wide or narrow focus, but the central aim should be that as the child develops increasing mastery of the processes and skills, he or she has a greater freedom to organise and plan the work.

At upper junior level

By the end of the primary phase, the gifted and talented pupil should be capable of producing a topic which comprises a series of indexed chapters illustrated with well-drawn pictures, maps or diagrams.

At the secondary level

At the secondary phase, the gifted and talented pupil should be expected to employ the skills they have acquired and develop them in general curriculum assignments, and in individual or group tasks which are chosen by the pupils themselves.

Any evaluation of a pupil's work should be guided by two overall aims: firstly the evaluation of the child's ability with reference to the peer group, so that a child who has ability will be recognised and challenged; and, secondly, the importance of praising the child by indicating specific good points in the work, and giving advice about ways of tackling problem areas more effectively.

Some ways to evaluate work outcomes

Vocabulary and use of words
- Is the language appropriate to the subject?
- Does the work show evidence of a wide and sophisticated vocabulary?
- Does the work reveal that this vocabulary is used effectively and with clear understanding of the meaning of the words used?
- Are technical terms used correctly and appropriately?
- Is the meaning of each sentence clear?
- Are complex sentence structures used where appropriate?
- Is the style lively and interesting?
- Is the use of words and organisation of the texts more advanced than one would expect from a pupil of this age?

Analysis, evaluation, judgement
- Does the work show an understanding of all the issues involved – are they clearly set out and explained?
- Is it factually correct?

- Where there is conflicting information, is it clearly explained why one version is chosen, or is a convincing synthesis made from the information available?
- Is the evidence supporting any judgements made clearly set out and evaluated?
- In discussion does the pupil show an understanding of the limitations of the work and further issues which need to be explored?
- Does the work reach a conclusion?
- Has a suitable range of sources been consulted for the subject to be fully discussed?
- Are consulted sources of a suitable level of accuracy and authority?
- Are biased sources identified?
- Has the treatment of the subject been imaginative without being fanciful?
- Was the work well planned and executed?

Conceptual understanding
- Does the writer understand the subject?
- Are difficult ideas well expressed, making matters discussed clear rather than obscuring them?

Logic and rigour in reasoning
- Are there any obvious gaps or mistakes in reasoning?
- Have the sources been accurately interpreted?
- Do the sources support the arguments?

Synthesis of complex ideas
- Have the strands in an argument been effectively examined?
- Has the evidence been successfully blended into a cogent argument?

Reading level required by sources
- Were the topics chosen and the sources used of a level appropriate to the pupil's age and perceived ability?

Confidence
- Did the pupil approach the topic in a businesslike way?
- Is the style of writing appropriate to the subject?

Commitment to task
- Is there evidence that the pupil has attempted to deliver the best possible product and has given it the maximum care and attention?

Clearly evaluations of pupils' work are more complex as they progress through the school system. However, teachers should not be afraid to rely on their own judgement in both recognising gifted and talented pupils and monitoring the progress they make.

It may be that some will find the criteria offered above too complex or confusing. However, the general headings should be enough to allow them to design their own evaluation scheme. What is really important is that the attempt should be made, and increasing experience and systematic use will refine the set of useful criteria and, more significantly, help to develop a greater understanding of what constitutes high-ability performance in this area.

Published material particularly for gifted and talented pupils

Infant materials

The units of the Macpack Infant Project ('Stamps and the Postman', 'A Room of Your Own' and 'Shopping') produced by Newcastle LEA would provide an excellent starting point for early years teachers. They not only encourage children to find things out, but also present them with practical tasks and problems to solve. An analysis of the good points of this material should help teachers in the task of designing their own units. They are also excellent for diagnosis of children's abilities and encourage cooperation and sharing of ideas. Similarly, the Essex Infant Project packs on Air, Early Man, Snails and Dinosaurs are full of very useful materials.

Junior materials

There is a further selection of topic booklets, about the Weather, Maps, Native Americans, etc., from Essex LEA which can be augmented by the delightful cross-curricular units from Crosslinks. Able Children also produce a growing range of junior project materials. Some of the Humberside packs can also be used at this phase.

Secondary phase materials

In addition to some first-rate Essex units, there are the Humberside packs and projects for Able Children. The now defunct Tressell Cooperative produced some excellent materials, some of which may still be in existence in some schools and should still prove very useful.

However, the materials available need to be augmented by units that have been produced or modified by teachers in individual schools or in local authority working groups – a process that was discussed in an earlier chapter.

References

Callow, R. (1997) 'Resources for the able child', *Support for Learning* **12**(2), 74–7.

CHAPTER 9

Problem solving as a resource

Problem solving is an effective way of challenging gifted and talented pupils. Their interest is often gained by posing a question that is intriguing, and sustained by the motivation to puzzle something out. It can also involve different modes of thinking. A distinction is sometimes made between 'convergent' and 'divergent' thinking, prompted respectively by closed and open-ended questions; the former lead to 'right' answers which are the anticipated answers, the latter to those that are unexpected but still in their own way 'right'. There is obviously a link with the different 'types' of ability discussed earlier. The distinction is a useful conceptual one, though in practice convergent and divergent thinking very often go side by side.

Competence in solving problems is possibly the most important ability the human race possesses, distinguishing us from creatures who operate more or less solely on instinct and impulse, and from the higher primates who can perform successfully on a limited range of problems by trial and error methods. Its importance has been stressed time and again by great thinkers like Karl Popper, scientists like Sir Herman Bondi (1992), and writers like Krutetskii (1976), but the education system seems strangely unmoved, and increasingly the trend is towards the factual, banal and dull elements of schooling.

In identifying children of high ability, problems offer the teacher an immensely valuable resource – if it is properly applied. As Anita Straker wrote (1983:15):

> The child with a quick mental facility, who can see pattern and build on known facts to help solve problems, is showing indications of mathematical potential. This kind of child copes well with formal practice work, as do most children, but it is when they are given problems to solve that one sees the difference.

This is true not only in mathematics but in all other areas of the curriculum. As Russell observed (1956: 25):

> A problem is a task which a child can understand but for which he does not have an immediate solution. Problem solving, accordingly, is the process by which the

child goes from the task or problem as he/she sees it to a solution which, for them, meets the demands of the problem . . . [it is] behaviour which is more directed around an obstacle and towards a goal than are other types of thinking . . . Problems can be practical or speculative . . . A child must be able to understand a task before it is a problem to him/her . . . Schools . . . sometimes require a child to do work which they do not understand. In this case the problem is probably best described as a 'puzzle'.

A simple model for problem solving

Problem recognition: identifying the problem posed by unexplained circumstances.

Goal definition: this involves a clear statement of the initial problem and what constitutes a satisfactory solution.

Information collection: this could be through experiment or analysis of books, maps, diagrams, plans, pictures, etc., and involves assembling material that directly bears on the problem in hand.

Hypothesis production: the creative 'brainstorming' stage which attempts to assemble as many relevant ideas as possible without evaluation.

Selection of the most effective line or lines of enquiry: this is a more convergent stage, when moral, legal, economic and practical criteria are applied to find the most suitable line to pursue.

Solution: it can be a gradual step-by-step process, involving a number of forms of attack (discussion, experiment, etc.), or it can involve one single 'moment of truth'. Solving problems is like trying on suits of clothes to get the correct fit. At the end it may be that the conclusion is that there are a range of alternative options, one single effective solution or no practical solution at all.

Examination of the solution for its implications: what are the likely outcomes? What are the costs? What might go wrong? This stage also may involve both divergent and convergent thinking.

It is clearly impossible to give a definite description of how people solve problems, but it is possible to produce a model that isolates certain skills which can be taught and certain attitudes which can be encouraged.

As indicated above, such a model should allow for the possibility of a number of possible solutions or none, or for the conclusion that the only possible solution is worse than the original problem. The third stage obviously links with the first skill of information processing, and the later stages could be used for discussion of the moral, ethical or economic considerations.

An analysis of the simple model could produce a list of sub-skills to be developed and supportive attitudes to be encouraged.

Problem recognition

Skills	Processes
Ability to identify anomalies	(a) transactional reading
	(b) listening
	(c) observation
Ability to identify gaps in knowledge	(a) summarising
	(b) constructing matrices
Ability to identify logical fallacies	(a) syllogisms
	(b) use of Venn diagrams
	(c) use of symbolic logic etc.
Ability to apply imagination and critical faculties	(a) projection: what if?
	(b) examination of present situation
	(c) examination of ideal situation
	(d) description of realistic situation

Ability to recognise circumstances or facts that need explanation

Attitudes	Curiosity
	Sensitivity
	Openness to ideas

Goal definition

Identify significant factors	By introspection or experiment
Ability to examine problem from all aspects	By introspection or experiment
Ability to identify type of problem	(a) mathematical
	(b) logical
	(c) theoretical
	(d) practical
	(e) ethical/moral, etc.
Ability to formulate objectives	(a) clear expression
	(b) elimination of inessentials
Selection of area of attack	With respect to objectives and what is already known

Ability to identify areas for clarification	(a) asking general questions (b) asking specific questions
Ability to identify links with previous problems	(a) making generalisations (b) identifying similarities and differences (c) identifying patterns (d) identifying type of problem
Attitudes	Honesty Confidence Application
Information collection	

Communication	(a) choosing appropriate medium:
	  • writing
	  • drawing graphs, maps, diagrams
	  • model-making
	  • photographs
	(b) organisation of information under relevant headings
	(c) style
	(d) vocabulary
	(e) spelling and punctuation
	(f) correction of errors, by revision

Attitudes	Intellectual honesty Perseverance Confidence
Hypothesis production	
Hypothesis formulation	(a) organising information (b) selection of main elements of problem (c) openness to ideas and information (d) seeing problem from different aspects (e) fluency of ideas and expression (f) discussion
Hypothesis testing	(a) judgement using multiple criteria, i.e. moral, ethical, logical, social, economic, etc. (b) identifying weak chain of reason

	(c) emotional detachment
	(d) accepting unwelcome/contrary information
Selection of lines of approach	(a) deciding on objective criteria
	(b) weighing evidence
	(c) identifying false lines of attack
Attitudes	Confidence
	Openness to ideas
	Awareness of possibility of:
	• multiple solutions
	• no solution
	• no practical solution

Selecting lines of enquiry

Hypothesis testing	(a) experiment
	(b) introspection
	(c) discussion
	(d) trying particular cases
	(e) trying related problems
	(f) generalising from experience
Selection of line of attack	(a) organising information
	(b) selection of main objectives
	(c) selection of style of attack
	(d) selection of resources
	(e) selection of information
	(f) identifying snags
Systematic approach	(a) breaking problem into parts
	(b) control of variables
	(c) careful recording of results
	(d) efficient note taking
	(e) efficient retrieval
	(f) search for relationships
	(g) analysis of relationships
	(h) focusing on specific aspects
	(i) reformulating problem
	(j) making generalisations
	(k) working backwards
	(l) checking all working
	(m) using one solution to find others
	(n) evaluating progress

Attitudes	Confidence
	Perseverance
	Honesty
	Objectivity
	Ability to cope with failure
	Ability to accept contrary information
Solution and examination	
Evaluating solution	(a) compare with objectives
	(b) retrace steps
	(c) examine on basis of moral/ethical criteria
	(d) examine possible other solutions
	(e) test in parallel cases
	(f) test against other possible solutions
Examining possible outcomes	(a) examine best outcome
	(b) examine worst outcome
	(c) cite possible exceptional cases
	(d) examine effect on related areas
Decision making	(a) examine evidence
	(b) examine own decisions for bias or subjective reasoning
	(c) make summary of evidence
	(d) make decision

Clearly this model does not, in itself, present a teaching programme, and any attempt to teach the elements in a linear progression would not be successful. The ideas can, however, be used to inform a teaching programme. Problem solving is an activity that relies on the teacher's ability to build the child's confidence – to encourage trial and error and speculation: it is not something that can be 'delivered' but is to be nurtured in an environment which, in Weber's (1978) phrase, is 'safe'. The key element in the process is discussion between teacher and child:

It is essential that a teacher should listen to any spontaneous comment from a child, and try to assess the degree of understanding revealed by it. If he is halfway to the discovery, she needs to ask the question that will lead to it. If he has arrived, she needs to find out whether he can generalise the discovery by applying it to other cases. She has to estimate the intellectual leap of which each child is capable. She has to refrain from 'telling' when he seems to have reached a dead-end, and from depressing him by expecting too much and being disappointed. With the appropriate words and gestures, she challenges the able to further discoveries.

(HMI 1979: 5)

Even the best materials can be wasted by the 'delivery method'. The Lego Technic School Sets are excellent teaching aids, but if the children are simply required to complete the tasks on the cards in order, and the teacher merely monitors their performance, much of value will be lost. The activity is transformed, however, if the teacher intervenes directly, as this example will illustrate.

One of the early cards (Figure 9.1) requires the child to build a model with two wheels, which are free to rotate and are joined by an elastic band. The model is intended to illustrate a simple method of power transmission. A pair of children would normally work at this task. When the model is complete, the teacher asks: 'When you turn the first wheel, what happens to the second?'

Children:	'It turns.'
Teacher:	'Why?'
Children:	'Because the rubber band turns it.'
Teacher:	'Do the two wheels turn the same way?'
Children:	'Yes.'
Teacher:	'Why?'
Children (illustrating with a finger):	'Because the wheel and the band move in the same direction' (and they show the teacher so this is clear).
Teacher:	'When you turn the first wheel, does the second wheel turn the same distance?'
Children:	'Yes.'
Teacher:	'Are you sure?'
Children:	'No, we just guessed.'
Teacher:	'How could we make sure?'

This is discussed, and it is agreed that both wheels should be marked and, as one child turns the first wheel ten times (say), the other child will count the turns on the second. The teacher leaves them to do this and then, when the task is completed, asks: 'Well?'

Children:	'The second wheel only turns about nine and a half times every time we try it.'

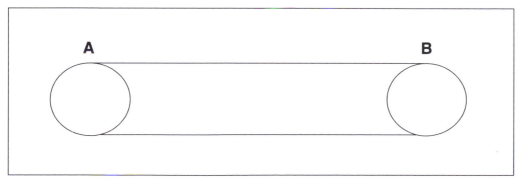

Figure 9.1 The model is intended to illustrate a simple method of power transmission.

Teacher: 'Why?'
Children: 'The wheels slip' or 'The rubber slips' or 'The rubber band stretches.'

The teacher congratulates them and asks two further questions:

'Could you think of a way we could test whether it is slipping or stretching that causes this?'
'If you cross the band over will both wheels turn in the same direction, and will the second wheel still turn less than the first?'

And so the process goes on. The children are learning to develop a hypothesis and test it and, perhaps more importantly, that the obvious answer is not always the correct one, that ideas can be challenged, and that experimenting is interesting and a useful activity.

Gifted children using this material, and with thoughtful input from the teacher, can explore ideas, experiment and generate their own problems. It also illustrates the effectiveness of the 'discovery method' if it is actively implemented.

The teacher's supportive role could be illustrated in the following example which is again drawn from experience gained. The problem is quite a well-known one and some readers may already know the answer. If this is not the case, it might be helpful to attempt to find a solution before reading further.

The Crystal Palace, a great structure of iron girders supporting a roof and walls composed entirely of glass, was built in Hyde Park to house the Great Exhibition of 1851. Unfortunately, it enclosed many trees and shrubs which were the home of flocks of sparrows, which soon made quite a nuisance of themselves. Queen Victoria became concerned about the matter and asked the Duke of Wellington how the sparrows were to be eliminated.

When this problem was given to gifted nine-year-olds, the responses usually went as follows:

Child: 'Get some men with guns to shoot them.'
Teacher: 'Yes, that would be quite effective, but have you considered what gunfire would do to the glass walls and roof?'
Child: 'Poison them.'
Teacher: 'Poison would normally be a good idea, but it does present certain dangers to the visitors. There were cafes in the building and it would only need a sparrow to drop some poisoned bread into a pan of soup to cause trouble.'
Child: 'Poison gas might work.'
Teacher: 'Another good idea: gas would be effective in an enclosed space. Unfortunately, the building did not have a modern ventilation system and it would be very hard to get rid of the gas once it was used.'

Child:	'What about cats?'
Teacher:	'Some sort of predator would probably be the most effective means. Would a cat be able to reach all the high parts of the building?'
Child:	'A flying cat.'
Teacher:	'Very good – a flying hunter.'
Child:	'A bird – an eagle or a hawk – a sparrow hawk.'
Teacher:	'A sparrow hawk would be the most effective.'

The first answer – 'shoot them' – reveals that the child has defined the objective as killing the birds; a response that indicated the intention of trapping the birds and releasing them elsewhere would be equally valid, and could be discussed with the child as a more humane alternative.

The process is one of gradual resolution of the problem by looking for the best 'fit'. No answer is wrong or silly; it simply redefines the problem or eliminates an unproductive line of enquiry. If a particular child appears to find the answers 'by magic' without any systematic approach, do not worry about this – find them more challenging problems!

These criteria may be difficult to apply in many cases since, as I indicated above, exceptionally gifted children will find answers to some problems so rapidly that no step-by-step approach is appropriate.

Evaluation of child's performance
- Speed in processing information and grasping the nature of the problem
- Ability to apply methods and ideas drawn from other disciplines
- Fluency of ideas and the ability to express them clearly
- Ability to think logically and in sequence
- Application to the task
- Willingness to abandon an unproductive line of enquiry and switch to another
- Ability to generalise from errors and successes
- Ability to devise short-term strategies for tackling specific groups of problems
- Ability to see the implications of the results and to criticise own conclusions

---

You have to accept this, and be careful not to try to impose your way of approaching the problems on the child if he/she is succeeding. Since many gifted children's minds can leap straight to the correct conclusion, without appearing to give it any thought at all, if they get the right answer (provided they know why it is the right answer) they should not be expected to show their step-by-step working.

Some useful problem-solving materials

At the infant stage

The Lancaster Materials are useful at the infant stage, once children have reached the requisite skill in reading. But clearly in the early years the emphasis must be on concrete activities, such as jigsaw puzzles, sets problems, and directed activities with construction sets: simple blocks, or the excellent but expensive Bau-Play materials, or the Lasy sets.

Tactical games, like noughts and crosses, chess, draughts and Fox and Geese, are of great value. One very important source of ideas is to be found in Martin Gardner's series of Mathematical Puzzles and Diversions books, and there are many useful materials in the Tarquin catalogue.

At the junior stage

All of the above can also offer much to the primary teacher, who will also find Anita Straker's (1983) *Mathematics for Gifted Pupils* essential reading as it provides a practical handbook of guidance on methods and materials. Able children produce problem-solving materials for this age range – to which can be added Able Pupils' Project Materials, Junior Thinklab, The Somerset Thinking Skills Project, Top Ten Thinking Tactics and the outstanding Lego Technic/Dacta materials.

At the secondary phase

SATIS Science and Technology materials and Longman's Mathematics through Problem Solving units bridge the phases, as do the role-play booklets produced by Penguin called Fighting Fantasy. These are carefully programmed texts allowing the player to attempt a specific task in a number of ways, by giving a choice of options and strategies. Pupils around the age of 12 find them interesting and exciting. They not only stimulate the imagination but also encourage creative problem solving. The equipment needed to play the game is simple – a book, some paper, a pencil and some dice. They need no marking but a discussion with the pupil about tactics and methods can be helpful.

There are two packs of Thinklab Problems and the CASE Science Materials for the Secondary Phase. Increasingly, however, the three processes – information handling, problem solving and self-expression – should become intrinsic elements of the ongoing assignments and projects that lead the pupils towards examinations and tertiary education.

There is a wealth of problem-based material to be found in games shops, on the shelves of bookshops and newsagents, and in the great sea of computer programs. Teachers can utilise these sources with increasing confidence if they have provided themselves with a clear set of objectives and criteria to inform their selection.

References

Bondi, Sir H. (1992) 'Why science must go under the microscope', *Times Educational Supplement*, 10 September.

Her Majesty's Inspectorate (HMI) (1979) *Mathematics 5–11*. London: HMSO.

Krutetskii, V. A. (1976) *The Psychology of Mathematical Abilities in School Children* (translated Teller, J.). Chicago: University of Chicago Press.

Russell, D. (1956) *Children's Thinking*. London: Ginn.

Straker, A. (1983) *Mathematics for Gifted Pupils*. London: Longmans for Schools Programme.

Weber, K. J. (1978) *Yes They Can!* Milton Keynes: Open University Press.

CHAPTER 10

Communication skills as a resource

The context of communication is closely linked with the way in which it is communicated. It is difficult to express bad ideas well. Conversely, high levels of thinking are best demonstrated by high levels of communication skills. The development of such skills is particularly important for gifted and talented pupils.

The ability to communicate one's ideas with clarity requires not only the ability to write and speak grammatically and the cultivation of good handwriting and punctuation, but also the ability to use words with accuracy and to master several styles of communication.

Elements of communication

Clear handwriting, good spelling and punctuation and a mastery of grammatical forms

Good vocabulary

Content organisation – the ability to organise the product into appropriate sentences, paragraphs and chapters

Clarity of language – presenting the product so that the meaning is easily understood

Mastery of different forms of written and verbal communications and an awareness of the audience who will receive them, e.g.:

- reports
- descriptions
- narratives
- instructions
- arguments
- discourse

Mastery of style – e.g. use of imagery, irony and awareness of shades of meaning and subtleties of language and argument

Deployment of content into an orderly and cogent sequence to secure the maximum impact

Skills of debate and argument, e.g. awareness of special pleading, bias, the half-truth, illogical conclusions, etc.

Editing material and rewriting it to improve style, tone and impact

Competence in other forms of information transmission, e.g. algebraic, mathematical and computer and Internet literacy

Competence in other human languages or machine languages

Experience of communication through art, music, drama and dance either as an initiator or a receiver

Competence in the critical appraisal of academic, imaginative, factual, graphic or dramatic works

Possession of creative ability which can transform most forms of communication

Once again, the elements appear in an order that is roughly hierarchical. Teachers should look for, and promote, the higher order communication skills with gifted and talented pupils. This, of course, applies across the curriculum and not simply in English.

Apart from the SAIL Project (Staged Assessment in Literacy) developed at Manchester University, there seems to be little material specifically directed towards developing communication skills. It is up to the teachers to develop their own programmes. These should be composed of three interrelated elements:

1. Presentation of examples of good communication.
2. Practice in a wide range of spoken and written communication.
3. Focused evaluation and discussion between teacher and pupils to develop their own critical skills.

Good examples

We can only appreciate what we know and it is, therefore, important that teachers take every opportunity to develop in the pupils an enthusiasm for the spoken and written word. In the primary phase they should tell them stories, read poetry or prose to them regularly, and actively encourage them to read widely by themselves.

Children should have the chance to absorb the rhythms of the language with choral speaking, and to develop a sense of the dramatic through watching plays and taking part in them so that the patterns and cadences of the language become so deeply ingrained that they become instinctive.

The first resource requirement then is for books: clean, well-produced, well-illustrated books of all sorts and descriptions, and in abundant numbers. Books are the basic building blocks of learning and civilisation and should be provided before thought is given to calculators or computers or links with the Internet, or any trendy item. They must, however, be carefully selected to ensure a wide spread of purposes and reading levels. It is important to realise that if one is serious about providing for the gifted and talented child, conventional notions of children's reading abilities must be modified. The gifted child of eight or nine is quite capable of reading seven or eight substantial paperbacks in one week and will most probably have a reading age of between 12 and 14 years, with an interest level perhaps a couple of years less.

There are many kinds of literature with many purposes:

(a) to inform (we have already commented on the need for good information books);
(b) to give a feeling of security and to entertain, e.g. Enid Blyton;
(c) to feed the intellect, e.g. philosophy, religious thought;
(d) to transmit many forms of human culture, e.g. legends and myths, ancient and modern history, science, music and art, religious faith;
(e) to feed the imagination, e.g. travel, fantasy, science fiction, adventure tales;
(f) to shape the emotions, e.g. poetry;
(g) to broaden awareness of self and others and the nature of society;
(h) to encourage self-motivated learning;
(i) to inform the style and form of personal writing.

It is perhaps even more important that secondary pupils have ready access to the best of modern literature as well as the classic English novels of Dickens, Austen, Hardy and Wells, Defoe and Fielding – and, similarly, to the playwrights from Shakespeare to Ayckbourn and Russell.

Practice

They need to be encouraged to evaluate their own products critically, to edit carefully and, where necessary, to rewrite.

The pupils in both phases need practice in the following forms of communications at the appropriate level:

- instructions
- description
- discussion – spoken and written
- argument

- personal interests and activities
- narrative – in prose and poetry
- expression of feelings.

Focused evaluation

Finally, the work must be evaluated in discussion with the pupil at every stage:

'Why did you enjoy this story?'
'Why did you use this particular phrase?'
'Would it have been more effective if you had put it this way . . .?'

so that the forms of literary evaluation become second nature to them. HMI (1979: 94) observes:

> Where teachers had recognised that talk was a means by which pupils could take an active part in learning, oral work was varied and more evenly shared between teacher and pupils. In such schools teachers did more than provide information and check to see whether the pupils understood it: they encouraged pupils to initiate discussion, to speculate and to offer differing views. Where these approaches were working well, and teachers and pupils had the appropriate skills and attitudes, they produced some valuable rigorous thinking.

The pattern, then, is at all levels:

- conceive
- write
- evaluate
- edit
- rewrite
- discuss

until both the pupil and teacher are happy with the result.

Criteria for evaluation of the pupil's product

1. fluency of ideas
2. fluency of language
3. choice of appropriate style for the purpose of the work
4. choice of appropriate language for the purpose of the work
5. wide and accurate knowledge and use of words
6. conciseness in expression of ideas
7. relative originality of ideas and presentation
8. lively and interesting style
9. ability to develop ideas and arguments logically and clearly
10. relevance of arguments and ideas
11. display of accurate and relevant knowledge of subject.

The two vital resources are books and the commitment and imagination of the teacher. It is desperately sad – at a time when a government can make a show of giving each child a book token (without reimbursing bookshops for them) – that school libraries are short of resources and the National Library Service is progressively starved of funds.

Resources

Well-stocked libraries and the enthusiasm and skills of the teacher are the most important resources, as has been indicated. There is little material otherwise which can be recommended. It remains for schools or individual teachers to develop their own sets of resources and techniques. Certainly many gifted teachers of English are indeed practising very successfully in this area, and their best work should be studied and widely published.

References

Her Majesty's Inspectorate (HMI) (1979) *Aspects of Secondary Education in England and Wales.* London: HMSO.

Organisations offering help, advice and courses for teachers, parents and children

The Able Child Centre

Calday Grange Grammar School, West Kirby, Wirral. Tel: 0151 625 3726.
(Offers a range of courses)

Centre for Talented Youth (Ireland)

Dublin City University, Dublin 9, Ireland. Tel: 00 3531 700 5634.
Fax: 00 3531 700 5693.
Email: ctyi@dev.ie. www.dev.e/ctyi

CHI

PO Box 21461, London N6 6WW.
UK Helplines (Help and advice for teachers and parents)
South – 01703 692621   London – 020 8693 2417
Midlands – 01386 881938   Nottingham – 01623 408157
Lancs. & NW – 01695 632563

Children's University

(Director: Anne Wood)
Martineau Centre, Balden Road, Harborne, Birmingham B32 2EH.
(Offers Saturday schools, holiday schools, distance learning. Caters specifically for
5–8 years) Email: wood.74@btinternet.org.   www.childrensuniversity.org
Tel: 0121 303 8294. Fax: 0121 303 8296.

European Council for High Ability (ECHA)

Bildung und Begabung, Kennedy allee 62–70, D.53175, Bonn, Germany.
Tel: 0049 228 959 1510. Fax: 0049 228 959 1519.
Email: bubev@compuserve.com

Gift

(Director: Julian Whybra)
5 Ditton Court Road, Westcliffe on Sea, Essex. (Courses for adults and children)

Mensa Foundation for Gifted Children

Mensa House, St John's Square, Wolverhampton WV2 4AH.
Tel: 01902 7722771.

NACE

(Conferences, courses, advice, publications)
PO Box 242, Arnolds Way, Oxford OX2 9FR. Tel: 01865 861879.
Fax: 01865 861880.
Email: info@nace.co.uk   www.nace.co.uk

NAGC (National Association for Gifted Children)

National Centre for Children with High Abilities and Talents, Elder House,
Milton Keynes MK9 1LR.
(Works with pupils, parents and teachers, annual journal *Gifted and Talented*,
newsletter)
Tel: 01908 673677. Email: amazingchildren@nagbritain.org.uk

NASEN (National Association for Special Educational Needs)

NASEN House, 4/5 Amber Business Village, Amber Close, Amington, Tamworth
B77 4RP. (Publishes a magazine *Special!* and two journals, *Support for Learning*
and *British Journal of Special Education*, yearly conferences. Has an interest in all
special needs, including the gifted and talented with special needs) Tel: 01827
311500.

NRICH

University of Cambridge, School of Education, 17 Trumpington Street, Cambridge CB2 1QA. (Online maths club for early teens)
www.lqts.norfolk.gov.uk/enrichment

World Council for Gifted and Talented Children

18401 Hiawatha Street, Northridge, CA 91326, USA.
(World association for educationalists, parents and gifted children, newsletter, journal *Gifted and Talented International*, regional conferences, world conference every two years)
Tel: (+1) 818 368 2163. Email: worldgt@earthlink.net   www.worldgifted.org

Books and sources of information for teachers

Burton, L. (1984) *Thinking Things Through: Problem Solving in Maths.* Oxford: Basil Blackwell.

Denton, C. and Postlethwaite, K. (1982) *The Identification of the More Able.* Oxford: Oxford Educational.

Evans, L. and Goodhew, G. (1997) *Providing for Able Children: Activities in Primary and Secondary Schools.* Dunstable: Framework Press.

Eyre, D. and McClure, L. (eds) (2001) *Curriculum Provision for the Gifted and Talented in the Primary School.* NACE/David Fulton Publishers.

Eyre, D. and McClure, L. (2001) *Curriculum Provision for the Gifted and Talented in the Secondary School.* NACE/ David Fulton Publishers.

Fisher, R. (1998) *Teaching Thinking.* London: Cassell.

Freeman, J. (1968) *How to Raise a Bright Child: Practical Ways to Encourage your Child's Talents from 0–5 years.* London: Souvenir Press.

Freeman, J. (1979) *Gifted Children: their identification and development in a social context.* Lancaster: Medical Technical Press. Baltimore: University Park Press.

Freeman, J. (1991) *Gifted Children Growing Up.* London: Cassell. Portsmouth: Heinemann Educational.

Gross, M. (1993) *Exceptionally Gifted Children.* London: Routledge and Kegan Paul.

Kennard, R. (1996) *Teaching Mathematically Able Children.* Oxford: NACE.

Kennard, R. (2001) *Teaching Mathematically Able Children* (2nd edn). London: David Fulton Publishers.

Leroux, J. and McMillan, E. (1993) *Smart Teaching – Nurturing Talent in the Classroom and Beyond.* Ontario: Pembroke Publishers.

O'Connell, H. (1996) *Supporting More Able Pupils.* Desk Top Publications (6 Silver Street, Winteringham, Scunthorpe DN15 9DN).

Renzulli, J. S. (1995) *New Directions for the School-Wide Enrichment Model,* in Katzko, M. W. and Monks, F. J. (eds) *Nurturing Talent; Individual Needs and Social Ability.* Assen, NL: Van Gorum.

Robinson, N. (1996) 'Counselling Agendas for Gifted Young People: A commentary.' *Journal for the Education of the Gifted* **20**, 128–37.

Straker, A. (1983) *Mathematics for Gifted Pupils*. Harlow: Longman.

Teare, B. (1997) *Effective Provision for Able and Talented Children*. Stafford: Network Education Press.

Tempest, N. R. (1974) *Teaching Clever Children, 7–11*. London: Routledge and Kegan Paul.

Wallace, B. (2001) *Teaching Thinking Skills Across the Primary Curriculum*. London: David Fulton Publishers.

Weber, K. J. (1978) *Yes They Can!* Milton Keynes: Open University Press (contains an excellent section on problem solving).

Local Authority and DfES guides

DfES

website: http://www.official-documents.co.uk/document/ofsted/veryable/able.htm
Educating the Very Able. 12 November 1998.
A very useful basic guide to the subject of gifted and talented pupils.
website: http://www.standards.dfes.gov.uk/excellence
A great wealth of information about the Excellence in Cities programme.

Ofsted

website: http://www.ofsted.gov.uk
Gifted and Talented Education appears in the special needs section.
Look out for *Providing for Gifted and Talented Pupils: An Evaluation of Excellence in Cities and Other Grant-funded Programmes*. Ofsted 2001.

QCA (Qualifications and Curriculum Authority)

website: http://www.qca.org.uk
Look for *Schools – Providing for Gifted and Talented Children. Identifying Talented Pupils*.

Guidance for teaching gifted and talented pupils is a website section of guidance for teachers, coordinators and others involved in teaching gifted and talented pupils. It appears in the Inclusion area of the National Curriculum website (*www.nc.uk. net/gt/*). The site includes specific guidance for each National Curriculum subject, as well as links to useful resources. General guidance on the site includes sections on identifying gifted and talented pupils, school and subject policies, the roles and responsibilities of the various people involved, managing provision, matching teaching to pupils' needs and transfer and transition.

Look for *Assessing Gifted and Talented Children.* ISBN 1-85838-490-7 (from bookshops).

Also look at *The Times Educational Supplement* website: http://www.tes.co.uk

Many local authorities involved in the Excellence in Cities programme have published guides which should be available on request.

The DfES officials concerned with the Excellence in Cities programme are very helpful and documents should be available from them if you do not have access to the 'web'.

Resources for education

This cannot be a complete definitive list of materials, for a number of reasons, and can only indicate resources that have been found to be valuable (some of which may no longer be available commercially but could still be in existence in school cupboards and bookshelves) and publishers who are currently producing materials that *could* be of value to individuals or groups of teachers and parents. The government initiative on Gifted and Talented Children has as one of its objectives the production of dedicated resources, but those with experience in curriculum development will understand that this will take a long time to accomplish.

As ever, it is the task of committed teachers to work with what is to hand to develop the intellect and skill of their pupils.

Publishers	Addresses	Materials
Able Children	13 Station Road, Knebworth, Herts. SG3 6AP Tel: 0138 812320	A wide range of materials across both phases.
Addison Wesley Longman	Pearson Education, Edinburgh Gate, Harlow, Essex CM20 2JE Tel: 01279 623928	Mathematics through problem-solving packs for 13–16.
Aquila Magazine	PO Box 2518, Eastbourne, East Sussex BN21 2BB	For pupils who enjoy a challenge.
Association for Science Education	College Lane, Hatfield, Herts. AL10 9AA Tel: 01707 283000	SATIS materials, science and technology for both phases.

Publishers	Addresses	Materials
Basil Blackwell Publishers	108 Cowley Road, Oxford OX4 1JF Tel: 01865 791100	The Somerset Thinking Skills Course by Nigel Blagg *et al.*
Bloomsbury Publishing	38 Soho Square, London W1D 3HB Tel: 020 7494 2111	Reading books.
BP Educational Service	PO Box 934, Poole, Dorset BH17 7BR Tel: 01870 333 0428	CASE Project.
Cambridge University Press Syndicate	The Pitt Building, Trumpington Street, Cambridge CB2 1RP Tel: 01223 312393	Mathematical activities books by Brian Bolt.
Chemical Industry Education Centre	University of York, Heslington, York YO10 5DD Tel: 01904 432523	Exciting science units and a wealth of other materials across both phases.
Claire Publications	Unit 8, Tey Brook Craft Centre, Great Tey, Colchester, Essex CO6 1JE Tel: 01206 211020	Maths problems for the primary phase.
Crabtree Publishing	c/o Lavis Marketing, 73 Lime Walk, Headington, Oxford OX3 7AD Tel: 01865 67575	Information books.
Crosslinks	The Bat, Falmouth Street, Newmarket, Suffolk CB8 0LE	Information books – a wide range of cross-curricular topics for the primary phase.

Publishers	Addresses	Materials
Dorling Kindersley Ltd	The Penguin Group (UK), 80 Strand, London WC2R 0RL Tel: 020 7010 3000	A large range of well-illustrated information books.
Essex County Council	Curriculum Access, Meadgate Centre, Mascalls Way, Great Baddow, Chelmsford, Essex CH2 7NS Tel: 01245 492211	Project units for primary and secondary phase specifically designed for more able children.
Evans Books	Sales Dept., 327 High Street, Slough, SL1 1TX Tel: 01753 578 499 Fax: 01753 578 488	Reading books, poetry, wide range of attractively produced information books. School presentations of materials can be arranged.
Folens and Belair	Apex Business Centre, Boscombe Road, Dunstable, Bedfordshire LU5 4RL Tel: 01582 470821	A wide range of primary and secondary materials. Creative materials in Belair list.
Fulton, David Publishers	The Chiswick Centre 414 Chiswick High Road, London W4 5TF Tel: 020 8996 3610 Fax: 020 8996 3622	Wide range of books on education. NACE publications.
Ginn & Co. Ltd	Linacre House, Jordan Hill, Oxford OX2 8DP Tel: 01865 888000	NCGM2 + NCGM6 + maths series for more able children.
HarperCollins	Westerhill Road, Bishopbriggs, Glasgow G64 2QT Tel: 0141 772 3200 Fax: 0141 762 0584	Vast range of readers from infant to adult fiction and non-fiction books on history, religion, science and Usborne range.

Publishers	Addresses	Materials
Hodder-Wayland	338 Euston Road, London NW1 3BH Tel: 020 7873 6000 Fax: 020 7873 6225	Wide range of fiction and resource/activity books across the age range.
Humberside Education Authority	Educational Publications, Coronation Road North, Hull HU5 5RL Tel: 0870 000 2288	Curriculum units on a wide range of subjects for both phases.
Kingfisher	Macmillan Distribution Ltd, Brunel Road, Houndsmills, Basingstoke, Hants. RG21 6XS Tel: 01256 302692	Readers and very attractive information books and encyclopaedia, largely for junior children.
Ladybird	Penguin Group Distribution Ltd, Bath Road, Harmondsworth, Middlesex UB7 0DA Tel: 020 8757 4000 Fax: 020 8757 4020	Reading scheme and attractive early readers. Unfortunately their well-illustrated information books, e.g. *Henry V, Alfred the Great*, etc. are no longer produced.
Lego UK	Ruthin Road, Wrexham, Clwyd LL13 7TQ Tel: 01978 236949	Lego Technic and Dacta Sets.
Macdonald Young Books	Sales Dept., 61 Western Road, Hove, East Sussex BN3 1JD Tel: 01273 722561	Information books.

Publishers	Addresses	Materials
Madeleine Lindley Ltd	Book Centre, Broadgate, Broadway Business Park, Chadderton, Oldham Tel: 0161 683 4400 Fax: 0161 682 6801	Reading and information books for Juniors.
Manchester University	Staged Assessment in Literacy Project (SAIL)	
McGraw Hill Book Co.	Shoppenhangers Road, Maidenhead, Berks. SL6 2QL	SRA Thinklabs I and II and Junior Thinklab.
Newcastle Education Authority	c/o Mrs Joan Lester, Ashfield Nursery School, Elswick, Newcastle upon Tyne NE4 6JR	Macpack Infant Projects.
Oxford University Press	Educational Supply Section, Saxon Way West, Corby, Northants. NN18 9BR	Reading and information books; Numbers, Shapes Revisited and What to Solve by Judita Cofman.
Penguin/Puffin	Penguin Group Distribution Ltd, Bath Road, Harmondsworth, Middlesex UB7 0DA Tel: 020 8757 4000 Fax: 020 8757 4020	Role-play books for top juniors and Martin Gardner's Mathematical Puzzles and Diversions, More Mathematical Puzzles and Diversions etc.
Qualifications and Curriculum Authority	Schools Providing for Gifted and Talented Children	KS1 and 2, English and Maths package with video and handbooks. A set should be available in LEAs.

Publishers	Addresses	Materials
Questions Publishing Ltd	27 Frederick Street, Hockley, Birmingham B1 3HH	Shakespeare for All files and Top Ten Thinking Tactics.
Reed Books Ltd	Reed Book Services, PO Box 5, Rushden, Northants. NN10 6XX Tel: 01933 414414	A wide range of reading and information books for the primary phase.
Shell Centre Publishing	Shell Centre for Maths, University of Nottingham, Nottingham NG7 2RD Tel: 0115 848 4476	Maths materials.
Spectrum Educational	Unit 2, Maskell Estate, Stevenson Street, London E16 4SA Tel: 020 7511 3129	What's in the Square? What Else is in the Square. Bauplay and Lasy constructional materials.
Stanley Thornes	Freepost (GR782), Cheltenham, Glos. GL50 1BR Tel: 01242 228888	Bright Challenge materials by Ron Casey and Valsa Koshy, and four problem-based maths enrichment books by Anne Joshua.
Tarquin Mathematics	Tarquin Publications, Stradbroke, Diss, Norfolk IP21 5JP Tel: 01379 384218	A large range of mathematical books, posters and apparatus.
Ward Lock Education Co. Ltd	Ling Kee House, 1 Christopher Road, East Grinstead, West Sussex PH19 3BT	Reading and information books.
Watts Publishing	96 Leonard Street, London EC2A 4RH Tel: 020 7739 2929	A wide range of reading and information books, both subject-based and cross-curricular.

Index